GW00367441

Self-Consciousness In Public

HOW TO CONTROL YOUR EMOTIONS

The Problem And Cure Of Self-Consciousness

EMBRACING

SELF-CONSCIOUSNESS. TIMIDITY. SHYNESS.
BASHFULNESS. BLUSHING. FEAR OF SELF.
FEAR OF AUDIENCES. CONTROL OF
EMOTIONS. SELF-RELIANCE. CON-
FIDENCE. CALMNESS. SELF-
POSSESSION, AND MENTAL
EFFICIENCY.

By
Dr. L. W. de Laurence

KESSINGER PUBLISHING'S
RARE MYSTICAL REPRINTS

THOUSANDS OF SCARCE BOOKS
ON THESE AND OTHER SUBJECTS:

Freemasonry * Akashic * Alchemy * Alternative Health * Ancient
Civilizations * Anthroposophy * Astrology * Astronomy * Aura *
Bible Study * Cabalah * Cartomancy * Chakras * Clairvoyance *
Comparative Religions * Divination * Druids * Eastern Thought *
Egyptology * Esoterism * Essenes * Etheric * ESP * Gnosticism *
Great White Brotherhood * Hermetics * Kabalah * Karma * Knights
Templar * Kundalini * Magic * Meditation * Mediumship * Mesmerism
* Metaphysics * Mithraism * Mystery Schools * Mysticism * Mythology
* Numerology * Occultism * Palmistry * Pantheism * Parapsychology
* Philosophy * Prosperity * Psychokinesis * Psychology * Pyramids *
Qabalah * Reincarnation * Rosicrucian * Sacred Geometry * Secret
Rituals * Secret Societies * Spiritism * Symbolism * Tarot * Telepathy
* Theosophy * Transcendentalism * Upanishads * Vedanta * Wisdom
* Yoga * *Plus Much More!*

DOWNLOAD A FREE CATALOG
AND
SEARCH OUR TITLES AT:

www.kessinger.net

Dr. L. W. D. Laurence

Copyright, 1916

By

de LAURENCE, SCOTT & CO.

Preface

This work has been written to meet the requirements of what the author knows to be a large number of people who suffer from a proper lack of Self-Control in public. In this class young men and women predominate, but close observation will demonstrate, to any one interested, that a large number of people of middle age are also included in this class which is greatly troubled with inward nervousness, bashfulness, blushing and timidity.

This *Volume* has been divided into *Two Parts:*

PART ONE is descriptive and *analytic;* the point of view is *genetic* and will be found strictly in keeping with the modern views of Practical Psychology and normal mental equilibrium.

PART TWO will be found to be the fruits of mature judgment, and the result of years of experience and observation of those peculiar mental states which beset one who is troubled with Self-Consciousness in public. The instruction given in PART TWO for overcoming the various forms of Self-Consciousness and Bashfulness lays down many laws and rules for combating the influences of fear; rules which the nervous individual, as well as the one who prides himself on his power of Self-Control, will do well to study and lay to heart. The efficacy of the principles enunciated in PART TWO can be depended upon as they are the result of the writer's extensive experience in his treatment of many hundreds of cases. He has also had the advantage of tracing good results from the methods, laid down herein, for the cure or control of the undesirable mental states, of those who have sought his advice for relief from excessive Self-Consciousness and Nervousness in public. This has enabled the writer to produce the present work, and to place it before the public with the knowledge that it will be the means of assisting a large number of people in overcoming their Self-Conscious fears.

The reader of this work is advised and admonished to pay strict attention to the advice given in the last paragraph of the Introduction. He * should first read through the book as a whole, marking with a pencil anything that applies to his case. He should next go through the book again, and read very carefully the portions penciled on his first reading. From a study of these he should draw up a plan or chart so that he may be able to carry out in a thoroughly systematic manner the instructions relating to his type of Self-Consciousness.

DR. L. W. DE LAURENCE.

------

* For convenience in writing, the masculine gender is used throughout in this book. All the rules, hints, and advice are, however, equally applicable to ladies.

CONTENTS.

———

iii

CHAPTER III.

SECONDARY CAUSES OF SELF-CONSCIOUSNESS.

CHAPTER IV.

SPECIAL CAUSES OF SELF-CONSCIOUSNESS.

Part Two.

CHAPTER V.

PRELIMINARY TRAINING FOR THE CURE OF SELF-CONSCIOUSNESS.

CHAPTER VI.

THE FEAR OF A CROWD.

CHAPTER VII.

TIMIDITY AND BASHFULNESS.

CHAPTER VIII.

THE NERVOUS TEMPERAMENT.

INTRODUCTION.

Several years ago, Mr. James Bancroft, a young man, was just beginning his career in a large business house, and one day was stopped in the street by a bank official, who enquired after the health of one of the members of the firm with which Mr. Bancroft was employed.

Startled by the suddenness of the inquiry, young Bancroft flushed up, his eyes filled with tears, his legs commenced to tremble, and it was with the utmost difficulty that he made a reply in a nervous, stammering manner. The bank official looked at him keenly, and recognizing his distress, passed on.

Mr. Bancroft was very much annoyed with himself. He had no *reason* to fear the bank official, unless *it* was the feeling of a difference in their social status, a difference which modern middle-class life is often at much trouble to distinguish, and to mark out with painful exactitude. And yet surely his whole attitude had been one of fear, or something very much akin to it; for how otherwise to account for the flushing of his face, the tears in his eyes, the loss of control over his limbs, and his nervous, stammering response.

He thought the matter over carefully, giving it great consideration. He had heard of people being self-conscious—was he self-conscious? Was the flushing, tearfulness, trembling, and halting speech, self-consciousness? *If so, it was truly a dreadful state of mind and body.*

The years passed on and Mr. Bancroft, under the personal direction of the author, made a careful study of the principles enunciated herein, until he gradually overcame his self-consciousness. After this he quickly acquired a full and exact knowledge of his business, until at length he secured a good position in his particular line of trade.

One day, in the ordinary way of business, he had occasion to call at a certain bank to see the manager on an important matter. He was taken into the manager's room and there sat the bank official, now manager, who had caused him so much distress at the commencement of his business career.

The wheels of time bring many changes. The manager of the bank was faced by an individual very different from the Mr. Bancroft of former days. Mr. Bancroft had acquired an attitude of strength, self-reliance, self-confidence, an atmosphere of self-possession, calmness and steadiness of manner, *that influenced all with whom he came into contact.* He had complete control over himself, and his words appeared to be measured out, and carefully adapted with a definite purpose to the matter in hand.

The manager of the bank was also a very different man from the young bank official of Mr. Bancroft's early business days. The vexations and worries connected with his position had told upon him. He was nervous, apprehensive, incapable of sitting still; he seemed ill at ease in the presence of this self-controlled, self-possessed man of business.

Mr. Bancroft felt with a sense of inward pleasure that their positions were now reversed. It was the bank-manager who was now distressed and showed the painful signs of the self-conscious state of mind.

How had Mr. Bancroft gained such control over himself? How had he conquered his self-consciousness? He had made a thorough study of the matter. *He recognized that it was as necessary to master the self-conscious state of mind as it was to master the intricacies of business.* He spared no effort, no expense, to acquire a knowledge of himself and the best means to control that self, and now he regarded that knowledge as his most valued possession.

Are YOU—you who read this book—*Self-Conscious* or *Nervous* in public? If so do you really wish to cure yourself of it? If you do wish to cure yourself, make a thorough study of this book and I guarantee success to your efforts if you carry out the principles laid down for your guidance.

* * * * * * * * * *

The reader is cautioned against merely selecting certain chapters of this book which touch upon his special difficulties and reading no farther. The Self-Conscious state of mind is so complex, the forms in which it may reveal itself so subtle, that it is necessary to get an all-around view of the subject. Only in this way will the individual get a good knowledge of himself and be able to grapple with his self-consciousness.

This book is written in TWO PARTS. PART ONE points to the need of *Self-Control* in daily life, indicates the obstacles to be overcome, and discusses the bad effects that *Timidity* has on one's efficiency. PART TWO instructs the reader how to secure that *Faith and Confidence* which is the chief characteristic of a *Strong Personality*. It includes, in addition, a series of practical Rules and Exercises to be used in overcoming *Self-Consciousness*.

If such a work as this is to do good, if the reader really wishes to benefit by the advice that it gives him, it must be read thoughtfully and diligently, not carelessly, and the reader must steadfastly keep before him the maxim of the *Author*—Personality is a power derived from the *"Mastery of Self."*

SELF-CONSCIOUSNESS IN PUBLIC.

PART ONE.

Self-Consciousness In Public.

Part One.

CHAPTER I.

THE PROBLEM OF SELF-CONSCIOUSNESS.

SECTION ONE.

WHAT IS MEANT BY SELF-CONSCIOUSNESS?

If you go to a dictionary for help in defining the word *self-consciousness* you will find it defined somewhat as follows: (1) *The act or state of being self-conscious;* (2) *consciousness, or awareness of being observed by others.* The first definition is so lucid that you feel you would like to make the acquaintance of the man who made it so that you might have the pleasure of stating your indebtedness. The second definition is nearer the mark, but you feel it is far from satisfactory.

Self-consciousness is primarily a thinking about the Self, but when you commence to think about your Self you find you cannot think of Self without bringing in the relation of that Self to other people. You begin to think of what other people think of you, or what you would like them to think of you. Your Self has no meaning for you without this extension—the bringing in of your relation to other men

1

and women. Self-consciousness, therefore, is mainly concerned with what other people think of us, or say of us, or what we assume they think or say of us. When our attention is fixed or concentrated on this relation of other people to ourselves we become self-conscious.

Now there are two ways in which self-consciousness manifests itself. (1) That of the person who takes pleasure in the thought that other people notice him, or note what he does or says. Sometimes, people of this class have grounds for thinking that other people are interested in their actions, etc.: in other cases the grounds exist solely in the imagination of these people. (2) That of the person to whom it is painful to think that others take notice of what he says or does. It is this mode of experience, where self-consciousness causes painful thoughts, that I seek specially to analyze. So marked is the painful element with some people that life is really a terror and a burden to them. I shall first, therefore, examine the causes responsible for the painful type of self-consciousness, and afterwards I shall prescribe the means of cure.

The reader is requested to note that in future whenever I use the terms *"self-conscious"* or *"self-consciousness,"* I am referring to the painful type of self-consciousness, never to the pleasing or pleasant type.

SECTION TWO.

THE CAUSE OF SELF-CONSCIOUSNESS.

A physician before he undertakes to cure certain ailments or complaints must first try to ascertain the causes of the complaints. He is faced with certain symptoms (an effect) ; he asks himself the cause. When he knows the cause, he has a basis on which to proceed to a cure.

Self-consciousness manifests itself outwardly as an effect —a highly complex state of mind and body. What is the cause of this effect? We know that in the nature of things there must be a cause for every effect, for cause and effect are one: they are distinguishable in form, but are identical in content.

If you were to ask an unscientific man to state the cause of self-consciousness he would probably correct you and say: "It it due, not to a cause, but to many causes." The doctrine of Plurality of Causes is still active with many people. With Mill they say: "Many causes may produce death," but this is a loose way of speaking. Death, here, is used in a general sense whereas the "many causes" refers to particular forms of death.

When I speak of self-consciousness I am using the term in a general sense, for there are many individual forms of self-consciousness, and each form has its particular cause. It is necessary that the reader should grasp this so as to have a better understanding of the cure of each form of self-consciousness.

I stated above that self-consciousness is a highly complex state of mind and body, and it is because of this complexity that it is impossible to give a general cure for self-consciousness. So many factors are involved that each must be examined in turn before it is possible to lay down rules for a cure of any particular state or type of self-consciousness. Again, it will be found that each type is complex; each involves several factors, and each of these has its cause and effect. Hence it is in the totality of these factors or conditions that the cause in its finality will be found.

To put it roughly, symbolically, the type of self-consciousness known as X involves the factors A, B, C. On examination we find A is caused by M; B is caused by O; and C is caused by P. To cure the condition X, we must lead up to it by curing A, B, and C, by removal of the causes M, O, P. This will be made clear as we proceed.

It is necessary, then, to keep in mind the fact that self-consciousness is a general term, and can, therefore be split up into individual, $i.e.$, particular types of self-consciousness.

In attempting to deal with these I will treat the subject genetically. To this end I shall state briefly the root cause of self-consciousness, the secondary causes (those arising out of the root cause) and special causes (those arising out of, or connected, in some way, with the root cause, and in relation to the secondary causes). I shall first outline these three divisions of the subject exhibiting their leading features; next I shall analyze them in detail; and finally, in PART TWO of this book, I shall consider the means of cure or control.

SECTION THREE.
THE ROOT CAUSE OF SELF-CONSCIOUSNESS.

Practically all who have studied the subject of self-consciousness are united in regarding fear, in some form or other, as the root cause of self-consciousness. This may be traced in the etymology of the word fear, which is connected with the idea of traveling. A fearer was a traveler, a person away from home, away from friends and customary sights and sounds. The unaccustomed brought with it the dawning of the Self and the relation of that Self to other things—other people, animals, things; the traveler had now become self-conscious.

It is easy to understand why fear must be regarded as the root cause of self-consciousness when we come to recognize the large part it plays in life. We fear evil men, disease, animals, things seen, things unseen and things non-existent, except in the universe of the imagination.

The abnormal fears of man have been classified under names that to the ordinary man are "fearfully" sounding. These fears are technically called *Phobias*. It is not necessary to detail all these fears, a few will suffice. Thus a common *Phobia* is *Agoraphobia*—the fear of open spaces, such as a field, a wide street, a square, etc.; Monophobia is the fear of being left alone; Mysophobia is the fear of infection from germs; Claustrophobia is a fear of high places; Siderophobia is the fear of railroads. These abnormal fears are often simple in origin. They may begin by reading or hearing about some experience in which such fears have played a part, or they may result from shock due to actual experience; but in essence they are alike in one respect— the person dwells on his fear until to think about it becomes a fixed habit.

The list of common fears is endless, for every new invention of science adds to our fears. We fear to go to sea lest the vessel be wrecked, we are afraid to walk along the street on a windy day lest a chimney-pot may fall. We fear to cross a busy street lest a motor-car or other vehicle may knock us down. We fear to go in a train—there may be a collision. We fear to go to a theatre or picture-hall—it may take fire. Fear surrounds us on every side if we pay heed to it and dwell upon it.

The self-conscious person has his special fears, and these concern us most. He fears himself, he fears crowds, he fears an audience when called to take the part of a speaker or performer (playing an instrument, acting, singing, etc.) He fears stage-fright and the dread of failure, he fears company (in social life), he fears interviews (applying for a situation, or for information), he fears people in business (his employers, heads of departments, and certain customers who come into relation with him in business), he fears responsibility and dreads standing alone or acting on his own initiative, he fears criticism and failure in anything he does, and lastly he fears the unexpected. From this list, which is by no means exhaustive, it will be seen how large a part fear plays in the life of the self-conscious person.

It may be objected that the fears enumerated above are not confined to self-conscious people. Before I answer this objection I must make it clear what I mean by self-conscious people. Ordinarily when you speak of or think of a person as being self-conscious you have in mind a person of the type of Mr. Bancroft in the INTRODUCTION. It should be noted, however, that self-consciousness is not always so marked as in the case of Mr. Bancroft; some self-conscious people have more self-control than others. Roughly, then, we may divide self-conscious people into two great classes; (1) The people who always seem self-conscious wherever we meet them, and (2) the people who reveal their self-consciousness only at special times, or on special occasions. It will be understood, I hope, that I use the term *"self-conscious"* in a universal sense so as to include both the narrow sense of the term, *i.e.* persons who know themselves to be self-conscious but are generally able to conceal it from others with more or less success; and the wide sense of the term, *i.e.* persons who *always* show their self-consciousness. Hence in answer to the objection above it should be noted that in the case of persons whom generally I should not speak of as self-conscious, in the presence of the special fears I have enumerated, they tend to become self-conscious; their self-consciousness, which ordinarily lies dormant, now reveals itself when brought face to face with these special fears.

SECTION FOUR.

SECONDARY CAUSES OF SELF-CONSCIOUSNESS.

The secondary causes of self-consciousness are closely related to the root cause. They may be classified as follows: —*Timidity, Shyness, Bashfulness, Stammering, Blushing.* These may be termed physical factors, as they are closely bound up in the nature of our being. Some of them are in fact hereditary and have come down to us from unknown ancestors.

There are two more secondary causes necessary to complete the list, namely, *Ridicule* and the *Ludicrous.* These may be termed mental factors, for they depend largely upon knowledge and experience. They affect a much larger class of persons than any of the physical factors, for even the boldest, the most courageous of persons will at times succumb to ridicule, or feel put out by being placed in a ludicrous position.

I shall examine each of the above causes in detail later on; at present it is sufficient to state them.

SECTION FIVE.

SPECIAL CAUSES OF SELF-CONSCIOUSNESS.

Under the heading of special causes of self-consciousness, we shall confine our attention to two great causes, (1) *Nervousness*, (2) *Adolescence*.

(1) It may be thought that I should have classed Nervousness under secondary causes, since surely Nervousness is due to fear. In a measure this is true—certain forms of nervousness spring from fear, but it is equally true that certain forms of fear are due to nervousness. A little consideration will make this clear.

Nervous people may be divided into three classes: (*a*) Those who through heredity are predisposed to nervousness, (*b*) those who are nervous through fear of some kind, (*c*) those whose nervousness is due to ill-health, shock, the abuse of stimulants, wrong living, etc. People of this class owe their fear to their nervousness; when the cause of their nervousness is removed, the fear induced by their nervousness disappears.

The nervousness of all these three classes can provide a basis for self-consciousness. This is seen clearly in classes (*a*) and (*b*); in class (*c*) as the nervousness of these people develops they dwell upon it, it is constantly in their thoughts —to think of it becomes a habit of mind. Then from thinking of their nervousness in relation to themselves, they come to think of it in relation to other people—they become self-conscious.

(2) *Adolescence is the great period in life when self-consciousness is at its highest.* It is then most difficult to control, as mind and body constantly react the one on the other, and, in consequence, the self-consciousness of the adolescent responds to the slightest stimulus. Adolescence has a close connection with the secondary causes of self-consciousness, as I hope to make clear when we come to examine it in detail.

I have outlined roughly the various causes of self-consciousness: it is necessary now to examine them closely. I strongly advise the student of self-consciousness to study carefully the analysis of each cause of self-consciousness, for by so doing he will grasp much more clearly the significance of the methods which I shall lay down, in Part Two, for the cure or control of each type of self-consciousness.

CHAPTER II.

THE ROOT CAUSE OF SELF-CONSCIOUSNESS.

SECTION SIX.

AN ANALYSIS OF THE ROOT CAUSE OF SELF-CONSCIOUSNESS.

Fear is one of the strongest emotions with which the human race has to battle. It is a universal emotion—the man who fears nothing is found only in the realms of the popular novel. It attacks the bravest spirits in some form or other; the soldier who goes boldly into battle tends to be nervous or filled with fear if called upon to take an unfamiliar part such as addressing an audience. To say that no one is exempt from fear is quite a different matter from saying that of necessity he must show his fear or give way to it. Some of the boldest men and women are well aware of their fears, and yet set out valiantly to give them battle.

There are certain characteristics of fear that are found in every man and woman, in the presence of that which causes their fear. (1) A tendency to run away, (2) trepidation, (3) hesitation, (4) a tendency to falter. Let us examine these characteristic marks of fear.

(1) The correlate instinct of the emotion of fear is the instinct of flight. When we see something that alarms or frightens us the instinct of flight instantly asserts itself. Men conquer this or control it many, many times in their lives, but they can always detect the presence of the instinct prompting them to action. The instinct of flight is accompanied by interference of the breathing and the action of the heart and by much physical and mental distress.

(2) Trepidation is a well-known characteristic of fear,

9

for very few (if any) of us get through life without making
its acquaintance. It is common to speak of doing something
with trepidation. Trepidation signifies to tremble. The
etymology of the word limits the trembling to the feet, but
when we suffer from trepidation we tremble in all our limbs
—the trembling motion extends from head to foot.

(3) The word hesitation is used in common speech to
signify indecision where there is the choice between alternatives. The hesitation which springs from fear is a matter
of feeling. It always bears the marks of physical and mental distress. When the instinct of flight receives a check
through the nervous disturbance of the system, we hesitate,
and there is a tendency to paralysis of movement. The
connection between hesitation and fear is often seen in conversation and in public-speaking. The speaker makes a slip
and hesitates; if the hesitation is attended with slight mental
distress the physical associates tend to appear. If the mental distress becomes more severe the nervous disturbance
brings on panic, terror, and a complete break-down.

(4) The tendency to falter is a characteristic of the fear
that attacks us in speaking—in ordinary speech and in
public speaking. It arises from mental agitation and attacks
the lips and the voice; it is with the utmost difficulty that
they can perform their functions.

One, or more, of the above characteristics appear in every
form of fear. Sometimes they are so marked that all can see
them; at other times only the individual concerned is conscious of their presence.

SECTION SEVEN.

FEARS THAT ATTACK THE SELF-CONSCIOUS PERSON.

In the Chapter on ''THE ROOT CAUSE OF SELF-CONSCIOUS-
NESS'' I drew attention to certain fears to which the self-
conscious person is specially liable. To give prominence

to these fears I shall enumerate them again and then examine them in detail, in the following order:

Fear Of Self, Fear Of Crowds, Fear Of Audiences,
Fear Of Stage-Fright, Fear Of Failure, Fear Of Criticism,
Fear Of Company (Social Life), Fear Of Interviews,
Fear In Business, Fear Of The Unexpected.

SECTION EIGHT.

FEAR OF SELF.

It seems a strange thing to say that a man fears himself. What can it mean? Simply that a man lacks confidence in himself. In many cases this lack of self-confidence is due to a constant habit of depreciating self, an underestimating of one's abilities.

The fear of self is very marked when a man has responsibility thrust upon him. A young man, perhaps of good ability, is offered a position much superior to the one he holds. It may be that in his new position he will have to take charge of an office with many clerks under him; or his new position may mean the control of hundreds of workmen, or the control of an army of travelers, agents, salesmen, etc. He shrinks from such responsibility; he is afraid of himself, afraid of the labor involved in such a position. He questions himself: *"Can I manage so great a number of subordinates; can I face the constant worry involved in such a task?"* "No! No! No!" comes back the answer from his poor shrinking self.

If you were to ask such a man his reasons for declining the position offered to him, he would not care to confess he was afraid to tackle it. He would say, probably: "The money is all right, but I should simply be worked to death," or "I don't like the people; they get out of you all they can and discharge you;" or again, "So and so is in their employ, and I know that if I went I should have a lot of trouble with him.''

A man of this type *will* sometimes confess that he is afraid to accept the position offered to him, but his confession is generally made to his wife or to an intimate friend. He is careful, however, to disguise his fear. He says he is afraid the work will be too heavy, the responsibility too great, etc.; it is very rare that he confesses his real fear—his fear of himself.

Sometimes this fearing man is forced by circumstances to accept the position, and then the chances are great that his fear will be exposed. One man of this type I knew well. He was a chief officer on a steamship, and was offered the position of captain. He was afraid to accept and yet he had no reason sufficiently good to advance for refusal of the position. Much against his will he accepted the position, but he did not hold it long. The responsibility was too much for him and he became insane. Yet this man was a most capable officer, an excellent controller of the men under his charge, *but he could not control his fears; he was afraid of—himself.*

Often a most objectionable feature about the man who fears himself is a habit of sneering at the people who have no such fears, the people with push, initiative and confidence. He is a born pessimist; he cannot see the good in himself, nor will he recognize it in others. And yet in some rare moment of reflection, this man will recognize and admit to himself that his abilities are greater than those of the man he allows to walk over him in the superior position. Then he says the other man has plenty of cheek, is a fool, and will surely come to grief. *He never sees the spirit of confidence that animates the other man.*

Thousands of men of good ability have this fear of self. Year after year thousands of good positions are refused through this fear. The fear of self is specially liable to attack the young. I ask all young men and young women to conquer this fear before it is too late; before it becomes a fixed habit.

SECTION NINE.
FEAR OF CROWDS.

By fear of crowds I mean fear of people in the mass. This fear is quite distinct from that of fear of an audience: there the fear springs from the knowledge that a man has a part to play with everyone watching all his movements, and taking in everything in connection with him. In the fear of the crowd, there is no such knowledge for the relation of the self-conscious person to the crowd is often purely imaginary.

The fear of the crowd can be looked at from two points of view—the active and the passive. In the former real grounds for fear often exist; in the latter the grounds exist solely in the imagination.

Looked at from the active point of view you have the crowd as hostile. Of this again there are two aspects, (1) Where you have done something to raise the anger of the crowd against you, and (2) where you have done nothing to cause offense to the crowd. Under (1) you have occasions such as great national crises. The people versus the aristocrats at the time of the *French Revolution* supplies an example. The attack of employees on an employer or his head officials during a great strike is another instance. Under (2) you have the attacks made on innocent people by gangs of hooligans or roughs, or where a crowd mistakes you for some other person against whom they have grounds for anger or resentment. Both (1) and (2) excite real, terrifying fear, in the great majority of cases; but from the point of view of self-consciousness they are not nearly so important as those cases where the fear of the crowd springs from imagination.

Looked at from the passive point of view, there are several situations in life where the self-conscious person fears the crowd, *i.e.*, any collection of people, in small groups or large bodies. Some of the commonest of these situations are, entering a public meeting or assembly—church, concert-room, theatre, a large shop or store; entering a public conveyance —street car, motor-bus, train, steamer; walking along a promenade, taking part in a procession, walking along a street or road and having to pass groups of people who are standing laughing or talking. These instances will suffice to illustrate the large scope there is for self-consciousness in the presence of the crowd. It is safe to say that there is not a man or woman who has not at some time or other, in situations such as I have enumerated, felt in some degree the tendency to self-consciousness. Very few people, for instance, can walk down the aisle of a church or across a concert platform, with the eyes of hundreds of people upon them without feeling a sense of uneasiness. In many people it causes real distress.

Next time you are seated in a train, especially a corridor train or electric train with long open carriages, look carefully at the people as they enter, and you will note at once their self-consciousness. In many instances it is very marked; merely to glance at such people is sufficient to make them turn their heads away, or to look cross or annoyed. The case is worse if you are with friends, all laughing and talking together. To look at the self-conscious person then is to make him think your laughter and talk is directed against him. At once he will flush up and look distressed, and sometimes he will seek refuge by going to another part of the train.

The fear of the self-conscious person, where the crowd is passive as above, is a real fear. The construction he puts on the attitude of the crowd towards him is, in the great majority of cases, the work of the imagination, but the fear in every case is real; a fear that causes distress to mind and body in varying degree.

The fear of the crowd, especially in its passive aspect, is

very prominent in adolescence, and where it exists in the adult in any marked degree, its origin can nearly always be traced back to the adolescent period. The reason why this fear is prominent in adolescence is easy to grasp. Adolescence, as I have already stated, is the period in life when self-consciousness is at its highest; it is the awkward age, the age when speech and the movements of the body are felt to be awkward by the individuals themselves. When, therefore, a boy or girl, or a young man or young woman is confronted with a crowd of people who are looking at them, or thought to be looking or laughing at them, the boy or girl, or the young man or young woman feels this keenly and shows his (or her) self-consciousness so that all may recognize it. Self-consciousness of this kind—the passive fear of the crowd, is easy to cure. I guarantee that no sufferer of this type of self-consciousness will fail to conquer his fears, if he will carry out the instructions given in PART TWO of this book.

SECTION TEN.

FEAR OF AUDIENCES.

Fear of an audience is of two kinds, (1) Fear prior to coming before the audience, and (2) fear when actually before the audience.

Fear prior to coming before an audience is due to what psychologists term prefunctioning. You imagine you see the audience. You see the platform or stage and you see yourself looking out from it on those hundreds of eyes, those cold, critical faces—somehow they always appear to you as cruel, sneering, mocking faces. Next, in your mind's eye, you are a dual personage; you sit among the audience and watch for the moment when you will see yourself stand there alone on the platform. You see yourself come timidly before the people, or with a rush as if you wanted to get your part over as quickly as possible. You note how awkward your platform figure looks, how helpless, timid, bashful, the legs shaking and trembling, the arms and hands lost for knowledge of what to do with themselves, the face drawn and anxious, the teeth chattering, the hair tousled, the clothes as if about to drop off. An then you see that awful moment when you fail, break down, and rush or scramble somehow off the platform, followed by the jeering, mocking laughter of the audience.

The more vivid your visualization of the scene, the more you give way to this prefunctioning, the greater is your agony of mind. You break into a cold sweat, there comes a sinking feeling in the region of the stomach, you shake and tremble and your entire nervous system is demoralized. You are a bundle of nerves—a jarring discordancy. With some people this perfunctioning is so real that it thoroughly unnerves them and they are compelled to back out of their engagements. Where an engagement is fixed for some weeks ahead the prefunctioning goes on day and night right up to the time of the engagement, with the result that many people are so unstrung on the day of the engagement that they are utterly incapable of doing justice to themselves.

Fear, when actually before an audience, may be of two kinds. You may be in the audience when suddenly you are invited by the chairman of the meeting to come on the platform and take a part in the proceedings. In such cases there is no time for prefunctioning, and you must either make up your mind quickly and take your courage in your hands or decline the invitation. A clergyman told me once that he never felt fear so keenly as when these sudden calls were made upon him. He would drop in at a meeting, seat himself close to the door, when suddenly in a pause the chairman of the meeting would look in his direction and say: "I am pleased to see our friend the Rev. Mr. —— among the audience; perhaps he would like to say a few words." This clergyman was extremely popular, and, simultaneously with the chairman's invitation, the audience would turn round and applaud vigorously, and in many cases this clergyman would have to go forward and make a few remarks in an utterly unprepared state of mind.

The other form of fear, when actually before an audience, shows itself the moment we step upon the platform to speak, sing, play, etc. There may have been prefunctioning, but we feel it is nothing to the actual experience. We realize that the real audience is more terrible than the ideal audience—the audience of our imagination. It is at such moments that stage-fright is apt to assert itself, and then the performer or speaker finds himself unable to do what he came prepared to do.

The greatest artistes, the greatest orators are not exempt from this form of fear. Great singers have said that the moment they came on the platform they felt the fear of the audience so strongly that it needed all their self-control and power of will to go through with their work. JOHN BRIGHT,* one of the greatest platform orators the world has ever seen, declared that he never came to a public meeting without experiencing a sense of fear. Popular clergymen have told the same story. At the moment of entering their church the fear of the audience has asserted itself so keenly that they have felt inclined to turn back, and run down a side street to efface themselves.

To people who have never studied the matter, this fear of the audience on the part of great artistes, orators, etc., is something they cannot understand. Why should these people who are supreme in their work feel this fear of an audience? The answer is simple. These people have a great reputation to sustain, and there is always the tendency to think they may fail to do well when they come in front of an audience. *A reputation is hard to gain, but easy to lose.* Hence the great artiste's fear that he may make some blunder or break down, and so ruin his career.

* John Bright, an English statesman.

This fear of the audience is the price that everyone must pay who seeks to do well before the public. Just as it is impossible to prevent thoughts from *entering* the mind, so it is impossible to prevent this fear of an audience from making its attack. But this is quite a different matter from saying we must give way to the fear. I have said we cannot prevent thoughts from *entering* the mind, but we can prevent our *dwelling* upon these thoughts. Likewise we cannot prevent the idea of fear of an audience from entering the mind, *but we can control the idea, and avoid dwelling upon it.*

A young clergyman once asked a great preacher how he could prevent this thought of fear in front of an audience from entering his mind. *"You cannot prevent it,"* replied the great preacher, *"and God help you if it were possible, for that same moment you would be lost—your power would go from you."* When we come to deal with the control of fear of audiences we will examine what the great preacher meant; and will show also, in more detail, how it is that this fear of an audience attacks the greatest artistes, orators, and performers, when they come before the public, and also what it means to them.

SECTION ELEVEN.

FEAR OF STAGE-FRIGHT.

The fear of stage-fright must be distinguished from the fear of audiences as outlined above. Stage-fright is a *sudden* fear and is liable to attack everyone, even men who have been for years accustomed to face an audience. Prominent men in the *United States Senate*, men in the front rank as speakers, have experienced this fear; in the middle of a brilliant speech stage-fright has come to them and left them incapable of further speech. The *Senate* or *House* notices a slight faltering, hesitation, then a sudden pause; the next moment they see, to their great astonishment, the brilliant speaker sit down thoroughly unnerved. Distinguished actors, musicians, preachers have all experienced the deadly fear of stage-fright.

Stage-fright always tends to paralyze movement and speech. It makes its attack suddenly, and is nearly always mental in origin; in cases when this is not so, it can be traced to some form of ill-health—being below par, nervous strain and tension, and so on. Where the cause is mental there comes the thought of failure. A slight hitch in the performance when playing an instrument, a slight faltering or hesitation while speaking is enough to start the fear of stage-fright. *"My memory fails me,"* "my strength will not carry me through this ordeal"—thoughts like these will start the fear. The thought that a deadly blunder has been made, or utterance given to some expression liable to be misunderstood by the audience, or to be accepted in a sense different from that intended, will start the fear.

When the fear of stage-fright once asserts itself it is characterized by the following features, (1) The tendency to paralyze thought, speech, and movement. Where this is not absolute we have (2) the tendency to hurry, to get through what we have to do as quickly as possible. The musician, conjuror, juggler, etc., hurries up his movements; the orator, speaker, actor commences speaking rapidly. Where there is a slight paralysis of the motor centers of speech, song, or movement of any kind we have (3) the tendency to confusion of thought, loss of memory—then follows rapidly, faltering, hesitation, floundering, mistakes, and finally a complete break-down.

When the victim of stage-fright gives way to the fear, and breaks down, the experience is always followed by terrible depression of mind. If he is a professional musician, or a public entertainer, he feels he must give up his profession and enter one less arduous. If he is an orator, or speaker he feels he must give up speaking in public. If he is a clergyman, he thinks he had better turn his attention to journalism, business, etc. In nearly every case stage-fright tends to make the victim depreciate his abilities, and to turn what talents he has into some other sphere of activity. In many cases the victim of stage-fright actually makes the exchange; in other cases, quiet reflection, the advice of a friend, the reading of an inspiring book, or the determination to succeed, shows the victim the folly of making the exchange. And then the world benefits, for in such cases he emerges from the ordeal, a stronger, better, all-round man.

I advise everyone who aspires to do anything in a public capacity to study carefully our remarks on the control of stage-fright in PART TWO of this book. The methods advocated have been well tested and can be recommended with confidence.

SECTION TWELVE.

FEAR OF FAILURE.

At first sight it may appear that the fear of failure has no relation to self-consciousness, but when you remember that this fear is one of the most potent causes of stage-fright, you will recognize that we are bound to give it some attention.

The fear of failure is of two kinds, (1) In its commoner form it is a check against enterprise and initiative. We fear to enter into new undertakings, fear to make a change, fear to take risks, for we fear failure. (2) In its second form the fear of failure comes to the man who is the direct opposite of the man with no enterprise. It comes to the man who is actively engaged in something. He may be a literary man, a business man, a speaker, a concert artiste, or an artisan engaged on some special task. In the midst of his work the fear of failure comes stealthily, or suddenly. It generally works by auto-suggestion: "*I don't think you will make a success of that.*" "*You are bound to fail—give it* up." "*You have made a terrible blunder—you have ruined your reputation.*" If you listen to auto-suggestions like these the fear of failure has an easy and sure victim in you.

The fear of failure is one of the greatest, if not the greatest, paralyzer of human effort that can be named. The world has lost much from this fear. Thousands of men of undoubted talent are engaged in humble, menial tasks, are occupying inferior positions simply through fear of failure; they are afraid to launch out into spheres of activity where their talents will have a chance to be recognized, and where their energies will have the stimulus that comes from congenial labor.

When the fear of failure attacks the worker it has the same paralyzing effect as in the case of the man who is afraid to enter on a new enterprise. It tends to damp his ardor, check his energy, and to paint everything as black as possible. When it comes to a man in front of an audience he loses his grip, gets confused, and in this condition is an easy prey to stage-fright.

The fear of failure, when the localization of functions is more advanced, will be found, probably, in a small cluster of nerve cells. These failure cells, if we may so term them, are sensitive to the slightest stimulus, ever ready to send up into consciousness the thought of failure. The failure cells have numerous associates, and as soon as they are stimulated, they pass on the nervous impulse to their associates with great rapidity until the mind as a whole is dominated by them. It will be readily understood that everything depends upon the nature of the stimulus. Where the call to action is immediate, the failure stimulus is so great, that the effect on the mind is practically instantaneous. In the case of a man called to do anything before the public, as for instance public speaking, entertaining, etc., the fear of failure generally makes its attack with lightning speed, and then we have the attendant fear of stage-fright, with its deadly paralysis of effort and movement.

The fear of failure in its commoner form is difficult to cure if it be of long standing, but it *can* be cured if the victim is willing to pay the price, and can be got to regard it in the right light. Once he recognizes that no advancement in life is possible until the fear of failure is conquered, he is ready to commence the cure. I shall show him, later, the path he must travel; it is a path that is rugged at first, but the pleasant places on the way are many, to the man who will keep steadily on.

With regard to the second form of the fear of failure, the hopes of cure, or more properly, control are very bright. *I cannot teach you how to prevent the thought of failure entering your mind, but I can show you how to control the thought, and how to prevent it affecting your career.*

SECTION THIRTEEN.

FEAR OF CRITICISM.

The self-conscious person has a great dread of criticism. A slight analysis of what I mean by criticism will reveal the grounds of his fear.

Criticism is a term that is used primarily in connection with literature and the fine arts, but it is used also in a much wider sense. To criticize signifies to judge; it is a weighing up for or against. A critic examines carefully the merits or demerits of a work, its beauty or its ugliness, its strong points or its weak points. A true critic gives his reasons for his judgment. He explains why he considers a work good or bad, beautiful or ugly. He must be scrupulously fair and free from bias. Criticism in its wider sense is a scrutiny of every form of human effort. We criticize books, pictures, music, with a facility born of ignorance. We criticize men, women, and children; we criticize their actions, their speech, their dress, and everything about them. In this wider and inexact sense, every human being is a critic.

With the self-conscious person—the extreme type—criticism is always regarded as an unfair thing, an unholy thing; it is a personal attack directed against himself, his actions, or his work. Even should the criticism be favorable, he is suspicious; it may be the prelude to a stinging attack, an attempt to lead him into more ambitious work where he may fail, and criticism may have a sure target.

The self-conscious person tries to avoid anything that will cause him to be criticized. He is afraid to take part in an entertainment in public, or to sing or play at a private gathering. He is afraid to enter public life lest everything he does or says may be unmercifully criticized. He is afraid to write a book lest it be noticed unfavorably. He is afraid to take an important position lest the way in which he conducts himself in the duties pertaining to his position be criticized. He is afraid to advertise lest what he says in his advertisements may be wrongly construed, and make him the butt of ridicule.

The real or basic reason for the self-conscious person's fear of criticism is the fear of ridicule, and the fear of the ludicrous. As we shall examine these fears in the section on "SECONDARY CAUSES OF SELF-CONSCIOUSNESS" it is unnecessary to do more than state this basic reason.

A certain type of self-conscious person bases his sole grievance against criticism on the fact that it brings him into notice, into prominence; this he wishes to avoid for he dreads to meet people, and to have himself discussed as if he were an object under a microscope. He shrinks from the notice of the public; he does not want it for he does not understand people; he prefers to go through life unnoticed, unsung.

I have said enough about the fear of criticism to show that it is a powerful factor in life. It is a fear that works untold mischief, for it prevents many a splendid man and woman from coming forward and doing good service to the world. Happily, its cure is not difficult if the matter is regarded fairly and squarely. If *you* are troubled with this

fear I guarantee to cure you, if you will follow the methods
I shall prescribe later.

SECTION FOURTEEN.

FEAR OF COMPANY (SOCIAL LIFE).

The fear of company springs from the fear of crowds,
i.e. people in the mass. It is a fear that causes great trouble
to the self-conscious person, and it is a fear that all of us
have experienced, for it is one of the trials of the adolescent
period, when it makes its attack without discrimination of
sex. Its attendant fears are the fear of ridicule and the
fear of the ludicrous.

In two of its aspects the fear of company is very similar
to the fear of an audience. Thus we have (1) fear prior to
going into company, and (2) fear when actually in company.

The fear prior to going into company is always attended
by prefunctioning, but it is generally quite distinct from the
prefunctioning in fear of an audience. We cannot visualize
the scene so well. In facing an audience we know what is
expected of us for we go prepared to play a definite part.
In company, there is always something we cannot foresee,
hence our prefunctioning is vague and dim. We visualize a
certain number of people, the introduction to them, sitting
down to a meal with them, and then, perhaps, taking part in
games of various kinds, or some form of entertainment.

The fear when actually in company is determined by the
people with whom we come into contact. If they are jovial,
good-humored, easy-going, the self-conscious person does
not feel his trouble so keenly. If they are stiff, formal, pre-
cise, ceremonious, he is keenly sensible of his self-consciousness. In company like this if he sees people whispering or
smiling and looking in his direction, he feels they are whispering about him, or smiling at some oddity of dress, manner, or appearance connected with himself. If he is called
to take a part in a game, and anyone happens to laugh, the

laugh is meant for him—of this he feels certain. When he sits down to a meal with the stiff formal type of company, the self-conscious person thinks that every eye is upon him. Merely for his neighbor to ask him a question is sufficient to cause him to flush up, while if someone farther up the table speaks to him or invites his opinion on some matter which all the company are discussing he feels ready to shrink under the table, or through the floor. If he is asked to propose a toast, or to reply to one, he is overwhelmed.

The fear of company is so common, its symptoms so well known that it is needless to discuss it at length. It is a fear to which everyone is liable, on occasion, as we shall see when we come to discuss the fear of the unexpected; it is a fear from which the boldest, the strongest, and the most self-possessed are not exempt. It is in moments like these, that the man of strong self-control realizes what agony of mind the fear of company must bring to the person who has no self-control, and is utterly at the mercy of his self-consciousness.

The cure of the fear of company, so far as it is an habitual state of mind when in company, is not difficult, but it cannot be attained in a week or two. There is no magic about it; it is simply a rational training of the will and self-confidence, on certain well-established lines. *The result is sure for anyone who will undertake this necessary training.*

SECTION FIFTEEN.

FEAR OF INTERVIEWS.

By interview, I refer specially to cases where you have to meet someone whom you have never seen before, or whom you have seen, but who is placed on a pedestal, as it were, in your thoughts, and with whom you have had neither converse nor any other relations. I shall touch, also, on those cases where you have met the person whom you are going to see, but have never had any dealings with him similar to your present errand, or where you have met the person whom you are going to see perhaps several times on much the same errand as your present one.

When the self-conscious person goes to see a man whom he has never met before, as in the case of a clerk who has applied for a situation by letter, and has been requested to call, he is full of fear. He wonders what type of person he will meet, what reception he will meet with, and with what subordinates he will have to deal before he reaches the great man. Questions like these fill his mind to overflowing and bring with them hosts of fears until the self-conscious person wishes he were dead, or that there were no such things as interviews.

If he has seen before the person he is going to meet, his fears center round his conception of him, his general idea of him. He has seen Mr. A. in the streets, in church, or at a concert, but what sort of man is he in his office? He may be a very decent fellow outside, but a fiend in business. The self-conscious man becomes afraid, and wishes himself through the ordeal.

Sometimes the self-conscious person has met the person he is going to see, has been introduced to him, and has had a little conversation with him. He is now about to call upon him to request a favor, and he suddenly recognizes that he knows very little about Mr. C. In cases like this, somehow or other, the self-conscious person always prefers or inclines to look at the bad points about Mr. C., or what he imagines the bad points to be. He is afraid Mr. C. is a very different man *really* from the man he met; he is sure to cut him off with a curt no—perhaps he will even refuse to hear him out. *Fears, fears, fears; how easy it is to imagine them in such situations!*

Our last interview is the common type, where a self-conscious person goes to see his doctor, lawyer, or clergyman, professionally, about some trifling matter, perhaps. He has met them before, often, but his present errand is slightly different from any he has had before. How will he be received? What will the result be? Or it may be that his fear of the interview is purely self-conscious. He is not thinking of his errand but of the interview itself. He hates to be shut up with these people; he feels he always makes a fool of himself, or thinks that they always think he is a foolish person. He has a sense of unease; he wishes he were going anywhere but where he is going.

Here you have the self-conscious person pure and simple, the man who dreads meeting other people; the man who always imagines other people are thinking of him, speaking about him, condemning him. Is his cure difficult? By no means, if he will follow the advice I shall give him later in PART TWO.

SECTION SIXTEEN.

FEAR IN BUSINESS.

The self-conscious person has many unpleasant moments in business, for it brings a class of fears peculiar to itself. I will mention a few. (1) The fear of an employer, or of those in superior positions in the firm, (2) the fear of customers, (3) the fear of responsibility, or of something going wrong, (4) the fear of rush periods (inability to get through work), (5) the fear of losing employment. There are hosts of other fears peculiar to each kind of business, but they are mainly off-shoots of the above and can easily be correlated by everyone for themselves. Let us take these fears in the order as given above.

(1) The fear of employers or of those who are above us in position in the same firm is a terrible fear to the self-conscious person. He thinks that the eye of his employer or superior is constantly upon him. When they approach him he is conscious of a trembling feeling in his limbs, a sinking sensation in his stomach, and a slight paralysis of speech which displays itself in faltering and hesitancy in his replies to questions put to him. If he has made a mis-

take in his work he dreads his employer's approach for he is sure his dismissal is at hand. If his employer speaks sharply to him he is miserable for the rest of the day. His fellow employees, when they note his fear, often add to it by cruel remarks. "There's trouble in store for you to-day, old man." "The governor is in a terrible wax to-day; look out for beans if he sends for you;" and so on. Remarks like these make the self-conscious person almost terrified to look up should his employer come near him. He hurries with his work, and in his hurry often makes absurd movements which draw the attention of his employer or superiors to him. He is glad when the working day is over, and he often goes home in a state of utter collapse.

(2) The fear of customers causes a great deal of trouble to the self-conscious person. He is specially afraid of the customer who complains, for there is always the danger of the complaint reaching the ear of his employer or the higher officials of the firm. Sometimes he feels sure these complaining people have a spite against him and wish to injure his position. Commercials of the self-conscious type fear the complaining customer for he causes them infinite trouble.

The fussy, and the don't-know-what-he-wants customer are also difficult to deal with. They have a habit of talking much or loudly, thus attracting the attention of officials (especially in a shop or store), and the self-conscious salesman has to deal with their difficulties under the watchful eye of a superior, who notes how he handles the customer, and often feels it incumbent to come forward and "to put in his oar," thus adding to the complexity of the case.

The haughty, unapproachable type of customer is a source of trouble to the self-conscious salesman, making him nervous and ill at ease. The haughty person, with his iceberg atmosphere, freezes up the salesman. He is uncertain how to address him, he is afraid to ask too many questions, he brings the wrong article in his confused state of mind, his movements become slow or flurried, and all the time he feels that the unapproachable one thinks he is a fool, and will leave him to go to the manager with a complaint.

It is unnecessary to extend the list of the types of customer met with in business. Each is a separate study; each provides new difficulties for the self-conscious salesman.

(3) The fear of responsibility has been dealt with already in No. 16, "FEAR OF SELF," but there it was mainly in relation to new positions. In business life you are all called upon at times to accept responsibility from which you cannot very well withdraw. Here are a few typical instances. Someone slightly above you in position takes ill, and you are called upon to take his place for the time being. You are sent out to try to secure a contract for your department. A theft has occurred in your department, and you are selected to appear at court as the principal witness in the case. You are sent to secure information about a new client, and on your information will depend whether your firm will give him credit. You are asked to supply the advertising department with material or suggestions for an advertisement relative to the goods under your charge. Any departure, like the above, from your normal everyday life is felt as a responsibility, and your self-conscious nature shrinks from this departure from the normal.

(4) The self-conscious person has a dread of rush periods, for they are connected with this fear of responsibility. If he does not get through his work in time, or get through it satisfactorily, he knows he is in for trouble. Further, at rush periods his employer and the heads of the firm are very alert, going from department to department seeing that the wheels of business are revolving at top speed. The self-conscious person is apt to make blunders at such times, not so much from the extra spurt demanded of him, but more because of the extra watchfulness and supervision of those above him in the firm.

(5) The fear of losing employment is common to the mass of workers. With the self-conscious person it has a direct

relation to his self-consciousness. He knows that it tends to make him confused, awkward, and foolish, at times. He is afraid his employer or superiors will note this, and give him his notice to leave. I have known men of this type who had an actual dread of pay-day, fearing that each one would be their last.

From what I have said of fear in business, I think it will be apparent that the self-conscious person has not an easy time in business. Many of his fears are imaginary, but others have solid foundations in fact. He is very suspicious and doubtful when you tell him his fears are curable, whether due to fact or fancy. His mental attitude is so fixed, so pronounced, that it is difficult to get him to change it. *His* case is always different from that of anyone else. I shall show him later that this is not so, that his case is similar to thousands of other cases. The lines of cure which I shall lay down will be broad, but they can be applied successfully to each individual case.

SECTION SEVENTEEN.
THE FEAR OF THE UNEXPECTED.

The fear of the unexpected reveals itself in two ways. (*a*) The fear that comes through the knowledge that the unexpected does happen to us, (*b*) the fear that arises through the actual happening or presence of the unexpected. It is necessary to distinguish carefully the difference between these two ways in which the unexpected makes its attack.

(*a*) This is either an ever-present fear, or a fear recurrent at special times or on special occasions; in the latter case it arises from numerous stimuli. It will be noted that (*a*) really amounts to an attempt to foreshadow the unexpected. Ordinarily this is not seen, for it is simply an apprehensive state of mind, but when it is attended by prefunctioning and imagination it declares itself, and may pass into actual dread of something terrible happening, or it may become in the ever-present form a fixed idea or obsession. When the fear of the unexpected passes beyond the limits of simple apprehension it easily passes into fear of the expected; something may happen and the attempt is made to determine what *will* happen. Such people when they go to a theatre, picture-hall, or other public place of entertainment, are always expecting a fire. If they go to sea, they expect shipwrecks, collisions, fire at sea, etc.

(*b*) The fear that arises from the actual happening or presence of the unexpected is the *real* fear of the unexpected. The other form is more properly an apprehension of the unexpected, or an attempt to see the unknown. (*b*) is properly the fear of the moment, the fear that comes through the presence of the unexpected, and its owes its power over us to the fact that it often catches us when we are unprepared, when we think that everything is going smoothly. This fear makes its attack with dramatic suddenness, and it spares no one—the bravest, the boldest, the strongest, the most self-possessed men and women acknowledge its power; and it has laid many of them low.

The fear that arises from the presence of the unexpected can come in many ways. (1) Through mistakes or miscalculations; (2) through happenings which you cannot foresee and over which you have no control; (3) or sudden news; (4) situations where you cannot foresee the issues; (5) unexpected callers. Let us look at these.

(1) (*a*) A dispenser to a doctor, or to a chemist makes up a bottle of medicine, and hands it to the patient, or sends it to the patient's home. Shortly after he finds that in error he has put a deadly poison in the bottle in a quantity that will mean death to the patient. Instantly the fear of what may have happened to the patient, should he have taken the medicine, attacks him. (*b*) A public speaker uses a word or phrase which as soon as he utters it he realizes is out of place. The sudden fear of what construction may be put upon it overwhelms him with confusion or panic. (*c*)

A general, in war time, has based his plans on the assumption that the enemy will follow a certain course. He discovers suddenly that he has made certain miscalculations; the fear of what may happen comes down on him with crushing effect. (d) A business man in an interview with a rival firm becomes aware that inadvertently he has "let the cat out of the bag;" he is filled with sudden dread as to what the consequences may be.

(2) Shipwrecks, collisions, fires, where no thought of these is in the mind, and where no danger from them is anticipated, supply common illustrations under this heading. We have seen, however, that certain people are always attempting to foresee such happenings, therefore it is necessary to examine a case where the happening cannot be foreseen, and is totally unexpected. The following case, which has come within my experience twice or thrice, will illustrate.

A violinist is playing a solo in public. Suddenly the accompanist's copy falls off the piano, and the audience laughs at his frantic efforts to catch it. The violinist, unaware of the pianist's mishap, hears the laughter, and thinks the audience is laughing at him. Fear seizes him, and he stops playing. When the pianist secures his copy and they commence playing again the violinist's grip of his solo is gone; the laughter and his sudden fear have made him self-conscious—*he has fallen under the spell of the unexpected.*

Other examples of fear from sudden happenings will be familiar to you through the newspapers, such as the sudden realization of being shut up in a railway carriage with a madman, the sudden attack of a vicious dog or wild animal, the danger of being run over, of having a close shave from danger.

(3) Business supplies many instances of the effect of sudden news in bringing forth the fear which comes through the unexpected. (a) A man buys a big parcel of shares on the Stock Exchange in the hope of a quick rise; all his judgment and expectation point to this. Next day to his astonishment

and alarm he finds that through the death of a wealthy man, a big holder of these shares, the market is flooded with the shares owing to the dead man's estate having to be realized quickly, and in consequence the price has dropped to a figure that will spell ruin to him unless there is a good rise before carrying-over day, for he cannot take up the shares. At once he is in the grip of the fear of the unexpected. (b) A man repeats to some acquaintances facts he has heard relative to the character of a certain individual. A few days afterwards he receives a solicitor's letter. He is appalled—the fear of the unexpected has made a deadly attack. (c) An editor puts an item of news in his paper which he regards as coming from a trustworthy source. When an action for libel is brought against him it brings with it the fear that comes through the unexpected.

(4) There are many situations in life where you cannot foresee the issues, and, therefore, the fear of the unexpected is easily aroused. Let us look at a few cases. (a) You receive a letter from a lawyer asking you to call. No particulars are given. You ask yourself: "What does he want?" You ring him up, but can get little satisfaction; the matter cannot be discussed except at a personal interview. (b) You receive a note from the Surveyor of Taxes asking you to call with reference to your return. What does he want, what has he discovered? A young clerk goes into a public-house at noon for a glass of ale. While he is drinking it the premises are raided by the police, who suspect the publican of using his house for betting. Everyone on the premises is arrested and taken to the police station. The young clerk must go too—what bearing will this have on his career if his employers get to know?

(5) Unexpected callers easily arouse the fear of the unexpected in many people. A ring comes to your door. You open it and find a policeman outside. A man calls at your office and begins to use threatening language, and gives every indication of a readiness to violence of action as well

as violence of speech. A young man away from home is giving a convivial supper in his rooms, when suddenly his father comes on the scene.

It is time now to examine the bearing which the fear that comes through the unexpected has on the subject of self-consciousness. I think it will be apparent that this fear tends through its very nature to rouse the self-conscious state of mind. It centers the attention on the *Self* and the relation of that *Self* to other people. Further, it tends to destroy courage, to make one frightened, timid, shy, confused, nervous. In some instances it brings blushing and stammering in its train. It always tends to paralyze thought and movement, to paint things black and gloomy, and to induce despair. The control of the unexpected, therefore, demands high qualities of mind, and a certain regime of *thought-control* to meet the sudden experience. Much, of course, depends on the individual's native endowment, but I can promise, when you come to that *Section* in PART Two which deals with the control of the fear of the unexpected, that you will see that much can be done to lessen the severity of the attack, *and surely that in itself is worth the acquirement.*

CHAPTER III.

SECONDARY CAUSES OF SELF-CONSCIOUSNESS.

SECTION EIGHTEEN.

AN ANALYSIS OF THE SECONDARY CAUSES OF SELF-CONSCIOUSNESS.

I have shown that fear is the root cause of self-consciousness, and have examined in detail some of the prominent forms in which fear tends to manifest itself. It is necessary now for us to analyze the secondary causes of self-consciousness, and to attempt to show how these are related to, or arise out of, the root cause. As these secondary causes play a most important part in the self-conscious attitude of mind, the reader is requested to give them special attention. The first of these special causes for examination is,

SECTION NINETEEN.

TIMIDITY.

It is not difficult to trace the relation of timidity to the root cause of self-consciousness; the etymology of the word shows this very clearly. Timidity comes from the *Latin* verb *Timeo*, "to fear."

It is necessary, at the outset, to distinguish between the words fear and timidity. Fear is an instinct, and is common to every human being. It is a state of mind called into being by a stimulus to which it is sensitive. From our analysis of various fears, we have seen that the stimulus necessary to arouse fear can come from many things, and from many quarters. Timidity is not an instinct; it is really a habit of mind, and like all habits, it reveals a process of growth. It grows from small beginnings until

35

it is rooted in the personality, and often completely dominates it.

The fear of the timid person is mainly imaginary. He imagines that certain persons conspire to make him ridiculous, to make him feel small, either in their own presence or in the presence of others. He is always on the look-out for signs of this conspiracy, and naturally he generally manages to find them. The timid person is terribly afraid of giving offense. His speech, his movements, his manner as a whole, proclaims this when he is telling you anything, especially if it is some item of news concerning yourself.

The timid person has very little command over himself. He is often lost where to put his hands and feet. He cannot stand erect and talk to you in the man-to-man attitude. His body is generally bent or stooping when in converse with his superiors, his articulation is indistinct, the tone of his voice low; he assumes a confidential manner, the don't-think-anything-about-it, I-hope-you-will-not-be-offended, manner. If he thinks you are *really* offended, or if you speak harshly to him, his timidity instantly gives place to real fear. He is terribly afraid of you. He trembles, his hands shake, his breathing becomes flurried and rapid, he flushes up, the perspiration rises on his brow —he is the embodiment of a man who is full of fear.

Timidity generally takes its beginning in childhood, or in the early years of adolescence, and is then often accompanied by shyness. The child's environment is often the cause of its timidity. Where a child is unduly repressed by its parents, brothers and sisters, or by its companions at school, initiative, individuality, and self-confidence are destroyed, and timidity makes its appearance. Again, when a child is an only child, and is not allowed much opportunity to play with other children, the timid habit has good soil in which to grow.

Timidity can be cured and overcome. This may sound "untrue" at first, to the timid person. I guarantee success, however, if the timid person will but persevere, and not mind a failure or two. I have known the rules set down herein to work wonders, turning the timid personality into one of strength and perfect self-confidence.

SECTION TWENTY.

SHYNESS.

Shyness, like timidity, is a habit of mind. It is not so much a fear of others as a fear of self, for the shy person is often a good fighter in debate, and can stick up for himself on occasion.

Shyness is really a shrinking up into self, a withdrawal from the presence of others. The shy person shrinks from doing anything in a public capacity, but when compelled to come forward, he often performs his part well, to the astonishment of himself and his friends. This is not to be wondered at, for shyness is often accompanied by real capacity and ability to do things. Many of the world's greatest men and women have suffered from shyness, but have been able to control it, or force of circumstances has compelled them to display their talents or genius to the world.

Shyness is often associated with great courage and great boldness, but these qualities of mind are generally latent with the shy person. He hesitates to display his courage or boldness; he wants to keep in the background. He shrinks from publicity, from coming to the front. He hesitates to give orders, and would rather do a thing himself than ask or command another to do it for him. The shy person suffers agonies of mind from this lack of courage, especially in connection with servants or subordinates. He is ashamed of himself, and it is only on occasion, when the stimulus is strong, that he can call up his courage and deal with the matter successfully.

The shy person is often a delightful personality—when

you get to know him, when he feels drawn to you, and feels you really understand him. He is grateful for your friendship, and highly appreciates your kindness, and your forbearance with him.

Shyness is often found in persons of great physical strength, people who, as we think, have nothing to fear from others, but in people of this type shyness is mainly associated with the fear of ridicule, and the fear of the ludicrous. Their very strength is really their weakness.

Shyness appears at a very early age. We say an infant is shy when it draws back from us and clings to its mother. It is probable, however, that this shyness is more due to fear, for the same tendency to run to their parents is seen in the young animals. Shyness is most prominent in the early or pre-adolescent period. The child feels that it is awkward, and shrinks from doing anything that may make this awkwardness pronounced; it shrinks from the risk of failure.

Shyness in adult life is due to many causes. It may have come down from childhood, it may arise from the consciousness of some physical defect, some facial blemish, some defect in speech; some secret sin (real or imaginary), from weakness or illness.

The cure of shyness is somewhat similar to the cure of timidity. The first stages of the cure are the most difficult, but once they are overcome, only a little perseverance is necessary to effect a permanent cure.

SECTION TWENTY-ONE.

BASHFULNESS.

Bashfulness is not a habit of mind; it is a state of feeling. I might suggest that it arises as a utility reaction on occasion of fear of persons, in view of personal qualities possessed by the one who fears.

Bashfulness is often associated with timidity and shyness, but its chief characteristic is a downcast look—a tendency to shrink from meeting the gaze of another person. In the adolescent stage this tendency is prominent with females, more so than with males. Sometimes this downcast look or air in a beautiful girl commends itself to us, and adds to her charms, but if there is great timidity with it much of the charm is lost, and we feel uncertain as to our approach. When this downcast look is seen in men there is no charm about it; we incline to call such a person sheepish.

In adults, bashfulness is seen mainly when in the presence of superiors. It is attended by flushing of the face, in some instances, and always with more or less confusion of mind. The bashful person often does himself great injury through this downcast air, especially if asking a favor or if applying for a situation. *Business men are not inclined to trust a bashful person; they often mistake his downcast look for stupidity or guilt; and they hesitate to engage such a person.*

Adults of the greatest genius and reputation are often attacked by bashfulness. A common occasion is when such persons are praised to their face, such as, for instance, when they are being presented with a testimonial, or when they are about to do something in a public capacity, and the chairman of the meeting or gathering indulges in eulogistic remarks. Many capable men detest such eulogy, and at once become bashful; they hate attention drawn to themselves instead of to what they are about to do. They regard praise as a distraction, and are afraid of it, for they know it tends to confusion of mind and interference with the work in hand.

In society, the bashful person feels excessively self-conscious. He is embarrassed, ill at ease, sensitive, is easily dismayed, easily frightened. His whole appearance seems to speak of lack of self-possession and self-confidence. *He is not a success, therefore, in society.* His humility, modesty and sensitiveness are often irritating to others, and cause them to have a false impression of him.

The cure of bashfulness must come through the control of the feelings. Where it is habitual, the cure takes time, but when it is only occasional, as for instance, when a person is praised before his face, the cure is not at all difficult.

SECTION TWENTY-TWO.

STAMMERING AND STUTTERING.

Stammering is such a well-known trouble that it is unnecessary to enter into a lengthy description of it. In brief, it is a defect of utterance, an infirmity of speech due to failure in the co-ordinate action of certain muscles and nerves whereby articulate speech is suddenly checked; the sudden stoppage is followed by hesitation and faltering as the speaker attempts to repeat the sounds. In mild cases the stoppage is slight, merely amounting to stumbling or faltering at unfamiliar words, or consonants of the explosive type, such as B, P, T, D, G. In some cases the stoppage is followed by a paroxysm of spasms of the muscles of the tongue, throat and face, with stoppage or difficulty in breathing.

Stuttering is generally regarded as akin to stammering, but it is not so severe in character. It is mainly a difficulty in pronouncing certain sounds. So far as my own experience of stutterers goes, their difficulty is mainly with the beginnings of words or phrases. This, too, seems to be the idea behind the etymology of the word, for it should be remembered that stuttering is an onomatopoetic word—one of that class of words formed to resemble the sound of the thing of which it is the name. The stutterer stumbles over the initial letters and syllables until after several attempts the whole word is exploded with more or less success. Stuttering is much easier to cure than stammering.

Stammering is due to two main causes, (1) A physical cause, (2) a physical, or mental cause. Some people include stuttering as due to these two causes, but personally, we incline to the belief that it is due purely to mental causes.

(1) Where the cause of stammering is physical, it may be due to (*a*) some obscure congenital defect, (*b*) some malformation—cleft palate, high-roofed mouth, disproportionate tongue or tonsils, (*c*) fevers or ill-health, (*d*) epilepsy, hysteria.

(2) Where the cause of stammering is mental, it may be due to (*a*) habit—a person may imitate a stammerer so well and so often that in time he finds it a habit with him, and more or less beyond his control. Children often acquire the habit in this way. (*b*) Mental strain or shock, (*c*) excitement, (*d*) the influence of strong emotions.

In the case of stammering due to physical causes, a complete cure is often impossible; the most that can be hoped for is an alleviation of the trouble. The cure of the physical type of stammering will not be attempted here as it does not come within the province of this book. I shall outline later some of the methods that have been employed, but with no attempt to dictate, or to influence anyone by them. Physical cases should be treated by a qualified medical man who has given the subject careful thought and study.

With the mental type of stammering, hopes of a cure are much greater. Psychologists incline to the belief that by far the greater number of cases of stammering are due to mental causes. I shall, therefore, in my cure section, give very special attention to this type of stammering.

Stammering begins in early youth; it rarely appears before the age of four or five years; the great mass of cases develop between these years and puberty—the early stages of the adolescent period. It should be remembered, however, that stammering, as we have seen in discussing its physical and mental causes, can attack one in many ways, as for instance in fever, ill-health, shocks, etc., hence stammering can make its appearance at any age.

SECTION TWENTY-THREE.

BLUSHING.

The normal man or woman who has never blushed is a phenomenon. The normal man or woman that nothing on earth can make blush is a still greater phenomenon. The person who asserts that he belongs to the latter class is either telling an untruth, or has never been put to the test.

Blushing is the most human of all expressions. It is common to every type of man or woman—the most highly cultured and the most highly educated, the man of no culture and of little education, the most civilized, and the most savage races.

It will be seen above that I doubt the existence of any man or woman who has never blushed, or that nothing can make blush. My reason for such doubt is this. The attack or stimulus can come in so many subtle forms that it seems to me folly to make such an assertion. It is one thing to say "I have never blushed"; *it is quite another thing to say* "I never will blush, nothing can make me blush." I shall make this quite clear in my examination of the subject.

There are four main types of blushing, or if you prefer it, four main ways in which we are liable to blush. There is (1) The blush of shame or humiliation, (2) the blush of anger, (3) the blush of love, (4) the purely self-conscious blush. Of the above types, (1), (2) and (3) require no explanation; the reader can easily imagine the situations in which they are likely to arise. The fourth type is more complex—it is the type that most people (who are concerned about blushing and its cure) have in mind when they think about the subject. Before we deal with it, we must look at blushing in its physical aspect.

Blushing is technically a *vasor-motor* phenomenon, a momentary paralysis or suspension of the *vaso-motor* nerve influence. It is the duty of the *vaso-motor* nerves to control the flow of the blood through contraction of the capillaries, thus preventing them from distending to their full extent. When the action of the *vaso-motor* nerves is suspended or interfered with through the power of an emotion, for instance, the capillaries become congested, thus causing that appearance of redness at the surface of the skin in the congested area.

Blushing usually effects only the head and neck, but it also, in rare cases, extends to the arms, chest, breasts, and lower parts of the body. The blush of shame commences at the cheeks and ears, the blush of anger first flushes the eyes, the blush of love flushes the forehead. The self-conscious blush floods the face and neck and gives one a feeling of great heat similar to that experienced when brought suddenly in front of a very hot fire.

There is an intimate connection between blushing and the sexual life, hence the reason why youth at the period when the reproductive functions begin to assert themselves are so greatly afflicted by blushing. The tendency to blush is much more common in women than in men, probably due to the greater complexity of their sexual life, and their innate sense of modesty.

Darwin regards blushing as hereditary; whether this be so or not it must be concluded that blushing is bound up with a great deal of our emotional nature, for instance (1) Love and the emotions surrounding the sexual life, (2) anger, (3) shame, and its connection with sexuality, and in its connection with social life—loss of prestige, disgrace, dishonor, anything in fact that shames us in the eyes of our fellows, (4) the mental states peculiar to the self-conscious person.

The self-conscious blush is peculiarly liable to appear in persons who are timid, shy, or bashful; it seems to make them its special prey. Especially is this so when any reference is made to their appearance, style of dress, any little thing about their person, or to their acts. Sometimes the slightest reference to any of the above, particularly the appearance, is enough to make the timid, shy, or bashful person blush. The reason of this lies in his extreme sensitiveness to notice, and as a person's appearance and dress often invite close scrutiny on the part of an observer, the self-conscious person shrinks from such scrutiny, and betrays his sensitiveness by blushing. Another reason lies in their fear of criticism; they are afraid that although the criticism may be silent, *i.e.*, not expressed, they may appear foolish, silly, or awkward in the eyes of anyone looking at them closely. Such close notice also makes the self-conscious person fear ridicule, of which he has a great horror.

The self-conscious type of blushing, in so far as it is a constant habit, can be cured, sometimes very easily. The methods of cure which I shall describe later are practical and founded on experience, and I can guarantee a cure, or a great measure of control over the habit to anyone who will follow these methods faithfully and persistently.

There is one point to which I must draw attention before closing this section, and that is the bearing of ill-health upon blushing. When a person's health is poor, it is often very difficult to control the tendency to blush, especially when any reference is made to his personal appearance, etc., as shown above in the case of the timid, shy, or bashful person. Even when such a person (I am speaking of the person in ill-health) has ordinarily considerable control, he is liable to blush under such circumstances. There is one consolation, however, and it is a great consolation; if he practice the methods described in this book, he will find that even should he blush on occasion, he will not be troubled with the mental distress and confusion of thought of the person who is ignorant of these methods of control.

SECTION TWENTY-FOUR.

RIDICULE.

Ridicule has such an immense bearing upon self-consciousness, that we must examine it very closely and at some length. At the outset I shall make it clear that the terms *"Ridicule"* and *"the Ludicrous,"* while they have much in common, are not synonymous—each has characteristics peculiar to itself, as will appear in my analysis of the terms. In this section I shall confine my attention to the term ridicule, and then the reader will appreciate better the distinction between the ridiculous and the ludicrous.

The word *"Ridicule"* comes to us from the Latin verb *Rideo,* "to laugh." In our use of the word at the present day it has, however, a much deeper significance than mere laughter. Ridicule always includes an element of criticism, for it is evoked by a strong sense of the absurd or irrational in that which excites our ridicule.

Ridicule is of two kinds. (1) That directed against persons, and (2) that directed against things. We may consider a person ridiculous, or we may consider something about him ridiculous. Thus a man may regard a lady's manner, bearing, or conversation as being ridiculous, or he may confine his attention to her hat, and call it a ridiculous hat.

Ridicule may be expressed verbally or in writing, as in a press notice or magazine article. Where that which excites our ridicule is slight or trifling, our ridicule is either good natured or mildly contemptuous. Where moral causes are involved, we have no feeling of laughter—our indignation is too strong for that; we condemn the person; he excites a feeling of contempt or disgust, and we turn away from him.

The above leads us, naturally, to note the distinguishing characteristic of ridicule; it always reflects upon the person to whom it attaches. It is this fact that makes ridicule have such significance for the self-conscious person. He knows that a person rarely appears ridiculous without really being so, and that he who is really ridiculous always excites our contempt. Hence his fear of ridicule, for he is constantly afraid of doing something or saying something that will excite ridicule, and thus cover him with contempt. Even good-natured ridicule, where displeasure is not in question, is terrible to the self-conscious person, for it draws attention to himself, and thus may arouse his tendency to blush with its consequent confusion of thought and action. He may then do things or say things that will make him truly ridiculous, and draw down upon him the scorn and contempt of all present.

There are many ways in which a person excites ridicule. We shall look at a few of these. He may excite ridicule by (1) His foolish pride, conceit, or eccentricities, (2) extravagant folly, (3) doing a thing awkwardly where skill is expected, (4) attempting something which he conceives within his powers, which nevertheless he is totally unable to carry through for lack of capacity. (1) and (2) do not concern us, since such persons, as a rule, are not troubled much with self-consciousness. (3) and (4), which have points in common, have a direct bearing upon our subject. *Let us look at them.*

Under (3) let us take the case of a pianist. Through ambition, he elects to play a certain solo in public. He has not played much of it until competent judges recognize that his technique is inadequate for a concert performance of the solo. He stumbles at difficult passages,

his fingering is scamped or uneven in runs, his touch in
cantabile passages is a burlesque. We feel his lack of
training, his thorough incompetence to do justice to the
solo; he, therefore, excites ridicule where he looked for
praise and applause. Or take the case of a conjurer,
who, instead of going to work in a deft, skillful manner,
bungles every trick. Here again, instead of applause he
calls down upon himself ridicule.

Under (4) the theatre, lecture-room and pulpit will
supply many illustrations of a person attempting something which he conceives to be within his powers, or
which is not in agreement with his personality or associates. Thus, when we hear an actor declaiming some noble
passage, the work of a great dramatic genius, in a manner
more suggestive of bathos than pathos, or when we see him
making love to a lady and eulogizing her beauty where
the lady has little or no claims to beauty, we call him
ridiculous, and we feel the situation to be ridiculous.
Again, when we hear a preacher giving utterance to some
sublime passage of scripture in a totally unsympathetic
manner, or with some peculiarity or defect of speech or
eccentricity of gesture, we feel disgust—he is ridiculous.

Now, self-conscious people are well aware of such ridiculous situations; they are keenly alive to them, hence
when they do anything in a public capacity they are
afraid that their audience will think of them in like manner, will think them ridiculous.

There is another situation I will touch upon where
ridicule may be said to be double-edged. It arises through
ignorance of the person who thinks another person is
ridiculous. A scientist makes a statement which to his
hearers is the height of absurdity, and they ridicule him
either verbally or by exposing him in writing. When the
scientist is right, and justifies his statement, the ridicule
turns on his opponents: the ridicule which they heaped
upon him falls on their own heads, and it is they who are
ridiculous.

The knowledge that ridicule is apt to arise from ignorance weighs strongly with the self-conscious person. He is afraid to make any show of learning in company lest his facts may be contradicted and considered foolish by the majority of his auditors. Likewise, where the matter is technical or uncommon, he is afraid to mention it lest it be beyond the comprehension of his auditors, and so excite ridicule.

I have said enough now, I think, to convince you of the power of ridicule. It is a weapon that everyone is called to fight against, if he is to do good work in the world. *In laying down rules for the control of ridicule, I shall give prominence to the needs of the self-conscious person.*

SECTION TWENTY-FIVE.

THE LUDICROUS.

In my examination of the ludicrous, I must, of necessity, make reference to the term *"Ridicule"* so as to bring out the essential difference between the two terms.

The word ludicrous is derived from *Ludus,* "a game," and signifies belonging to a game or sport. It carries with it a certain mental attitude—a fun-loving attitude, the desire to be amused, also the making fun of, or game of a person, hence the association of the word with laughter. When the laughter element passes into derision or contempt, the ludicrous gives place to ridicule.

The ludicrous is generally conceived as a situation in which we perceive sudden and unexpected relations, where things congruous or incongruous seem to meet, interchange, and fuse together. The essence of a ludicrous situation is always felt as an unexpected congruity in things which before were always classed as incongruous, and *vice versa* in the case of unexpected incongruities. Unless this perception of difference and agreement is felt in one act of thought, in one breath, as it were, there is no ludicrous situation.

We come now to the essential difference between the ludicrous and ridicule. Ridicule, when directed against a person, is always a reflection on that person; we hold him responsible for that which excites our ridicule. This does not hold in the case of the ludicrous. A person may appear in a ludicrous situation where no responsibility attaches to him. He may be entirely blameless, *i.e.*, the circumstances may be entirely beyond his control, and he comes out of the situation without any stain on his character, or any reflection upon his intelligence. It is this independence of the actor in the situation, therefore, that is the essence of the difference between the ludicrous and ridicule; without it there would be no perception of the congruous and the incongruous fusing into one element.

The feeling of the ludicrous can be aroused through persons, animals and things. Its relation to persons I will discuss fully, and in a lesser measure its relation to things. With regard to animals, it is necessary merely to instance the appearance of animals on the stage, or in circus performances, etc., where they are dressed up to represent human beings, and excite laughter through the absurdity of their appearance and actions.

Ludicrous situations may be of two kinds, (1) *The Real*, and (2) *The Unreal*. The latter is nearly always due to ignorance, and easily passes into, or allies itself with ridicule.

As illustrations of the Real situation, we may take the following examples :—

(*a*) A bishop, walking along a wet slippery pavement, suddenly falls in the mud and dirt. He rises with his hat damaged, and at a peculiar angle, or perhaps without his hat, which rolls away. His clothes are in soiled state with the mud, his hands are dirty, his face is bruised and partly covered with dirt. He is a sorry spectacle, and for the moment a ludicrous object. Even though our sympathy be aroused and active, we feel the ludicrous element, **for** instantly there arises in our mind two images; the image of the bishop's usual dignity and *mien*, and his present unfortunate appearance, more suggestive of a tramp or a hooligan. We at once feel the incongruity of the two images, and while we may sympathize with the bishop in his accident, we feel the tendency to laugh at his appearance, for we have the fusing of the two images into a congruous image—the image of an object that excites laughter. This is specially strong when we learn that he has suffered very little hurt from the accident.

(*b*) A well-dressed man, who gives one the impression of having a strong sense of his own importance, stops and looks in a shop window. Some mischievous boys seize the opportunity to pin to his coat a large ticket with the words *"Please kick me"* inscribed in bold characters. Here again we have the incongruity between the image of a proud, important type of person and the image of a buffoon, and the congruity of a laughable object. In both (*a*) and (*b*) there is no feeling of contempt or derision, nor is there any reflection upon the character of the individual concerned, since the circumstances are beyond their control, and we feel their independence.

As an example of the *Unreal* situation, take the movements or actions of a great pianist when playing a solo. The raising of the hands, the closing and opening of the fist, look ludicrous to a person with no knowledge of the relaxation of muscles in relation to piano technique. Or take the case of a person with very little knowledge of art, examining a great picture. It is ludicrous to him, perhaps, for it is beyond his comprehension, and not congruous with his ideas of art. In both these cases it is an easy step to pass from the feeling of the ludicrous to that of ridicule.

In all the examples I have given the feeling of the ludicrous is not mutual or common, *i.e.*, the situation is not felt to be ludicrous by the chief actor in the scene. Where the feeling *is* common, *i.e.*, where the situation strikes both parties, the actor and the onlooker as ludicrous, we have the comic, laughing element in the ludicrous strongly shown. A good example is that of the barrister in a well-known play of some years ago, who through an unfortunate and accidental exchange of traveling bags, rises in court, takes up his bag to draw out his legal papers connected with the case before the court, and draws out instead a pair of corsets. The scene is equally ludicrous to him and to the court, and although embarrassing at the moment, would no doubt have afforded him much amusement afterwards had it happened in real life.

The close connection between the ludicrous and ridicule is clearly shown in caricature. If the caricature is excellent in representation it excites the ludicrous, but if it is badly expressed, or goes beyond the limits of good taste, it becomes ridiculous.

The naturalness of the ludicrous, if I may so term it, where there is no attempt or intention to create the situation, is sometimes met with in the contents-boards of newspapers, or in a newspaper where the eyes pass rapidly from one headline to another, thus: "The Bishop Of X Indisposed—Due To Drink"; "The Senate's New Bill—Five Dollars And Costs"; "A Rising Dramatist—Hoist With His Own Petard." We feel the absurdity strongly in such cases, and they at once arouse our sense of the ludicrous.

Enough has been said in connection with the ludicrous to convince you that it is not nearly so deadly as ridicule. It is the failing of the self-conscious person not to be able to see this; he places both in the same category and on the same level. He fails to see that in the ludicrous there is no reflection made upon the actor in the scene, either morally or intellectually. If he will but grasp this clearly, he will be able to moderate his fear of the ludicrous. I shall go into this fully when I deal with the control of the fear of the ludicrous.

CHAPTER IV.

SPECIAL CAUSES OF SELF-CONSCIOUSNESS.

SECTION TWENTY-SIX.
AN ANALYSIS OF NERVOUSNESS.

In the Chapter on "SPECIAL CAUSES OF SELF-CONSCIOUS-NESS" we distinguish between nervousness due to fear and the fear that is due to nervousness. We also divided nervous people into three classes, (1) Those who through heredity are predisposed to nervousness, (2) those who are nervous through fear of some kind, (3) those whose nervousness is due to ill-health, shock, the abuse of stimulants, wrong living, etc. Classes (1) and (2) fall under the heading of nervousness due to fear, and class (3) falls under the heading of fear due to nervousness. A connection between classes (1) and (3) may be traced, but it is not necessary to go into the minutiæ of such connection.

Nervousness may be defined as a particular state of mind or body where the one interacts upon the other. Nervousness may be purely mental in origin, as for instance, where it is due to fear; or it may be purely physical in origin where it is due to infringements of the laws of health, or it may be due partly to physical and partly to mental causes through heredity. In the latter case we call persons so afflicted persons of a nervous temperament. These persons are predisposed to nervousness and as they form a large class in any community it will be necessary to understand what is meant by temperament, and next, all that is signified by a nervous temperament.

Popularly, a temperament is understood to signify a native endowment, peculiar to every individual, which is supposed to govern or color all his acts, all his thoughts, and all his feelings. The temperaments were formerly confined to four—the choleric, the melancholic, the sanguine, and the phlegmatic, temperaments. Moderns have added a fifth temperament, viz., the nervous temperament. The temperaments are never found pure in any individual, for they tend to coalesce and interact the one upon the other. Thus the nervous temperament is always associated with the sanguine, or melancholic temperament. We shall understand what this means later.

The nervous temperament is marked by great sensitiveness, great excitability, and great activity of the nervous system, with a strong tendency to emotional impulses and emotional excesses. It numbers in its ranks men of the highest genius, and has always played an important part in the history of the world in every sphere of activity.

The characteristic marks of a person of nervous temperament are intense activity of thought and movement. He talks quickly—volubly, or in jerky abrupt manner, and when his feelings are aroused, his speech is excited and often accompanied by gesture. He walks quickly, as if he had not a minute to spare, he eats his food quickly and suffers accordingly. In company he cannot keep still; he fidgets with his hands or legs, he cannot keep his head still, nor can he control his facial muscles, he is often worried to death, and is bad to deal with when ill.

It will be seen that this analysis of nervousness narrows nervous people into two great classes. (1) *Those whose nervousness is temperamental, and* (2) *those who cause their own nervousness.* As the latter is an important class with a strong bearing on self-consciousness, I shall examine it in some detail.

Medical men are fond of telling people that they live in a nervous age. The signs of this are easy to read. I will divide these broadly into general signs and individual signs.

General Signs. The nervousness of the age (I use the term age in its world-wide significance) are shown by a general feeling of unrest, a craving for excitement, novelty, and change. There is a hatred of monotony, a desire to get away from ourselves; we dread being alone, we must always be on the move. Panic is easily aroused; scare headlines in newspapers or on their contents-boards minister to the feeling daily. The Stock Exchange* was never so nervy—a puff of wind topples over or depresses mighty stocks and shares. Politics, religion, social life, business, are all full of nervousness. *The signs are broad enough for all to see.*

Individual Signs. The individual signs may be divided into physical signs and mental signs. The physical signs are restlessness, tremulousness, fatigue on slight exertion, pains in the head, giddiness, indigestion, nerve-sensitiveness, palpitation, low vitality. The mental signs are, inability to concentrate, lack of thought-control, erratic will-power, irritability, bad temper. The excitability of the nervous system is accompanied by emotional excess; there is a rush from one end of the scale of feeling to the other end, *i.e.*, tumultuous joy at one end and fits of depression and anger at the other. In women there is a tendency to fits of crying without any apparent cause. There is also a marked tendency to worry over trifles.

The Causes Of Non-Temperamental Nervousness. The causes of nervousness, where it is not due to a nervous temperament, are due chiefly to our mode of life in work or business, and to the ways in which we spend our leisure time. Business is done in a rush, it is fiercely competitive, and is full of daily worries, anxieties, and annoyances. All this works havoc with the nervous system, and when overwork is added to it, nervous breakdown results. Business is felt as a strain; it is a constant effort to forge ahead, and to "go one better." Workmen feel this rush and worry in

---

* This was written prior to the war between England and Germany.

their occupations. Work must be got through in a certain time and to do this means speeding-up with its consequent worry and anxiety. Professional men have to meet the same conditions of hurry and bustle with the added strain that springs from ambition—the desire to come out at the head of their profession.

With many people their business, work, or profession is felt to be monotonous; they find it a ceaseless grind day after day, hence the tendency to seek relief from their monotony in a whirl of pleasure after the toil of the day is over. The search for pleasure is responsible for all kinds of extravagant follies. Instead of quietly resting and taking things easy, men, many of them physically tired, go motoring, play golf, go on long motorcycle rides, or go nightly to places of amusement. The same strenuousness that marks their daily work is also a feature of their pleasures. As a result of this, insomnia is rampant, and the lack of sleep and the lack of rest have a destructive effect upon their nerves.

In social life the round of pleasures and engagements tell heavily on the nerves; women and men aim at the impossible—they try to do more than they are able to do, hence nervous irritability and emotional excess are common in this mode of life.

When nervousness gets beyond a certain stage it develops into a disease. Doctors call it neurasthenia, and its victims they call neurasthenics.

Neurasthenia. Neurasthenia, as its etymology shows, is nerve weakness. It is really a weakness of the nerve-centers. As will have been seen from what I have said of nervousness, it may be due to physical causes, or to mental causes. Its physical signs are stomach troubles, digestive troubles, muscular weaknesses, pains, flushes, chills, trembling. *Its mental signs are phobias, obsessions, morbid introspection, fear of insanity, a total inability to control the thoughts, and an imagination that runs riot.* When nervousness develops into the neurasthenic stage it demands treatment at the hands of a recognized, qualified mental-specialist. Only he is qualified to prescribe means of cure, for the complexities of these cases demand careful personal study of each case.

Nervousness, where it is due to a wrong mode of living, is not so difficult to cure as neurasthenic cases. Where it is due to temperament, much will depend upon the individual's ability to recognize himself as belonging to this type, *and his then endeavoring to conform to the rules I shall lay down.*

SECTION TWENTY-SEVEN.

AN ANALYSIS OF ADOLESCENCE.

In the Chapter on the "SPECIAL CAUSES OF SELF-CONSCIOUSNESS," I stated that adolescence was the great period in life when self-consciousness is at its highest. The reason of this is that it is then that the reproductive functions assert themselves and throw a tremendous strain upon the nervous system. The adolescent period for a girl is between the years of twelve and twenty-one; and for a boy between the years of fourteen and fifteen and twenty-five. These are the years of trial for a boy or a girl; they feel they are in a new world where all kinds of nervous ailments make their appearance. The functional changes makes the adolescent period a time of storm and stress for boys and girls; they feel the changed conditions keenly.

The adolescent period is marked by the following features, (1) Boys and girls tend to become awkward in their movements; the automaticity of movement is interfered with through conscious attention being given to the movement; the boy and girl *feel* they are awkward and lack their former grace and ease. (2) The voice changes, and again there is conscious attention paid to the change, with the result that the speech of the boy and the girl tends to become awkward, faltering, hesitating. (3) The awkwardness of movement and speech bring other troubles; boys and girls become timid, shy, bashful—they wish to efface themselves. In the presence of strangers, especially of adults, they feel unsteady, uncontrolled, fearful, and ready to shrink up into themselves. This is specially noticeable where the adult is calm and self-possessed. Boys and girls are keenly sensitive to the difference between the calm atmosphere of the adult and their own uncontrolled nervous state of mind and body. This difference of atmosphere is *always* felt, even where boys and girls have a fair measure of control.

The period of adolescence is the special time in the life of boys and girls when they require careful attention and watching, careful training so that they may come forth from this period of storm and stress, strong, self-reliant, and self-possessed, ready to do battle with the world. A great deal in this book centers round the adolescent period: *I specially commend the youthful reader to study carefully the secondary causes of self-consciousness, as they are the causes of self-consciousness which it is specially necessary for youth to grasp fully.*

SELF-CONSCIOUSNESS IN PUBLIC.

PART TWO.

Self-Consciousness In Public.
Part Two.

CHAPTER V.

PRELIMINARY TRAINING FOR THE CURE OF SELF-CONSCIOUSNESS.

In every branch of human effort, careful and prudent training is essential to secure good results. The bigger the aim in view the greater the necessity for a thorough grasp of fundamentals, and for careful graduated training. The self-conscious person is not exempt from this necessity: if he wishes to get rid of his trouble he must make up his mind to submit to preliminary training before attacking in earnest his particular form of self-consciousness.

SECTION TWENTY-EIGHT.
THE FIRST STAGE.

In PART Two it has been shown that fear is the root cause of self-consciousness, hence the first stage in the cure of self-consciousness must concern itself with the initial action towards the control of fear. I use the word *control* with purpose, for it is impossible to prevent fear from entering consciousness; *it is an emotion—an innate tendency—*and liable to arise from numerous stimuli. *Fear must be recognized—it cannot be ignored.*

Fear is a tremendous force in life; it can destroy, but it can also create; it unlocks hidden sources of power, and forces us to make the attempt to use them. This will be clear to you when you reflect that the correlate instinct of fear is flight. Now flight is really a call to action, a putting forth of all our activity to escape from that which causes us to fear. We must ask the self-conscious person to dwell a little upon this idea of fear being a force. Try to grasp that it is a call to action, a call to put forth energy. Remember that flight is not the sole channel of activity; the call is to *all* the powers of our organism. This is seen at once when there is a check to flight; at once the fighting instincts are aroused, and we give battle. *If victory crowns our efforts the seeds of self-confidence and self-reliance spring into life: we become bold, courageous, triumphant, dominant. As we become accustomed to this new state of being, we grow calm, self-possessed, fearless.*

From the above it will be apparent to you that the control of fear must begin with a particular mental attitude towards it. Try to look at fear as *creative*, not destructive, and at once you have your feet on the path of control. Learn that the weapons to fight fear are self-reliance, self-confidence, calmness, self-possession. With these at your command you have the fearless attitude of mind. When you know how to secure this attitude, you will find it easy to cure or control any type of self-consciousness. We must now turn to the second stage on the path you must follow to gain possession of the weapons with which to conquer fear.

SECTION TWENTY-NINE.

THE SECOND STAGE.

On entering the second stage of the path of control, keep in mind what the first stage has taught you, namely, that you must regard fear as *creative*. It is something that is going to arouse all the powers of your organism to fight against anything in the nature of an obstacle in any sphere of effort in your life. It must always be regarded as *a call to action*, never as a something that paralyzes effort.

This second stage is very important, for it deals with matters of fundamental importance. You must learn (1) The nature and use of inhibition, (2) how to control your muscles, (3) how to control your emotions—your feelings, (4) how to control your thoughts. At the second stage it must be understood that the rules I shall give will be general rules—particular or specific rules will be given, whenever necessary, later, in discussing the cure or control of each type of self-consciousness.

SECTION THIRTY.

THE NATURE AND USE OF INHIBITION.

(*a*) *Inhibition* is of such immense importance in relation to self-consciousness, that we must examine it with a certain measure of fullness.

It is customary to look at inhibition as simply a state of inactivity; something has been stopped, or prevented, and all further action forbidden. But this is to overlook the power that has caused the check or inaction. The truth is, inhibition is really a state of activity, a putting forth of energy to prevent some other form of energy from manifesting itself. Inhibition is, therefore, always dual in character; it always implies something done, and something prevented.

In the human body there are two kinds of muscles, voluntary muscles and involuntary muscles. The voluntary muscles (which alone concern us) are under the control of the will, and are generally arranged in pairs, each muscle of a pair being antagonistic in its action to the other. When one muscle is active the other is inactive, *i.e.*, it is inhibited. Thus, for instance, there are muscles that open the hand and muscles that close the hand; when the muscles that open the hand are active, the muscles that close the hand are inactive—both sets of muscles cannot be active at the same moment of time.

This rule of the antagonism of opposites extends also to the world of thought, or ideas. When you center your mind on one idea you oppose (inhibit) ideas antagonistic or opposite in character. Thus, you cannot love and hate a person in one act of thought, in the same breath, as it were. This gives the great rule for the breaking up of habits, and for all thought-control. To overcome the power of a thought you must employ another thought to drive it out.

(b) *The Value Of Inhibition.*—The value of inhibition is shown by the use to which it is put. Thus (1) It is the beginning of the training of the will, (2) it is the foundation of thought-control, (3) it is the foundation of all *psycho-therapeutic* treatment where will-power is at fault, (4) it is the starting point of self-denial, (5) it is a check to impulse, (6) it brings great and true benefits to the nerves.

From the above it will be clear to you that inhibition is the fundamental factor in the development of character. To the man who employs it constantly day after day, week after week, month after month, year after year, it will constantly reveal new possibilities.

(c) *How To Train Your Powers Of Inhibition.*—Begin the training of your powers of inhibition by simple little acts of denial or forbidding. First attack your desires, next your impulses, and then your thoughts.

(d) *How To Check Desire.*—You are accustomed to smoke a pipe, cigarette, or cigar every day, say after breakfast. Refuse to do it for *one* day, do something else instead. You are in the habit of drinking a glass of water, ale, wine, or spirits at lunch or dinner. Refuse to do this for *one* day—go without. You have a strong desire to go to a theater, or other place of amusement. Check the desire for *once*—do not go.

There are a number of little things which you are accustomed to do every day, or once or twice a week. Choose *one* of these little things each day, and refuse to give way to the desire which it expresses. *Do not choose the same thing every day;* the law of habit will be either too strong for you or the nervous disturbance will be too severe. By a constant change each day you are laying the foundation of your power of inhibition, *and you are training your will-power by easy stages.*

(e) *How To Check Impulse.*—An impulsive act is one that is done without thinking, without deliberation. The way, therefore, to check impulses is to think over quietly to what kinds of impulse you are liable, and to determine to check these in future. Your awareness of the impulse, and your intention to check it, are the lines of attack. When the impulse tends to manifest itself, your intention (made previously) to check it will rise at the same moment through association, repetition, and the law of habit. Many people have an impulse to steal, but every time the impulse rises there comes with it the thought of the consequences that may follow the act of theft, and hence they refuse to obey the impulse. By knowing the impulses you are liable to, and determining beforehand not to give way to them on their appearance, you will find that in time the check will manifest itself, automatically with the impulse.

(f) *How To Attack Unwelcome Thoughts.*—The rule for attacking unwelcome thoughts is simple. Every time the unwelcome thought arises switch your mind on to some other thought, *opposite in character.* Thus, if someone has done you an injury, switch the mind to someone of whom it is always pleasant to think, or if you at first find this difficult, set to work on some task that will engage the mind, and so shut out the thought of injury. The natural tendency of the mind to wander will help you, and you will find, with constant practice, that it becomes easier and easier to shut out disturbing thoughts. Do not mind a few failures. The law of habit will help you to conquer, if you will but persevere.

SECTION THIRTY-ONE.

HOW TO CONTROL YOUR MUSCLES.

When I speak of controlling the muscles, you will understand, I trust, that I refer solely to the voluntary muscles, as they are the only muscles that are under the control of the will. For the purpose of this book I will divide voluntary muscles into two classes, (1) The muscles of the head, trunk, and limbs, and (2) the facial muscles (as apart from the muscles controlling the movement of the head). For the student of self-consciousness, the facial muscles are by far the more important of these classes, and will therefore demand more attention.

(a) *How To Control The Muscles Of The Head, Trunk, And Limbs.*—It is unnecessary for us to enter into an elaborate system of rules for the control of the muscles of the head, trunk, and limbs. There are so many books and systems of physical culture which make a feature of this kind of control that it is needless for me to go minutely into the matter. All that I shall do, therefore, will be to give a few general exercises having a special bearing on our subject.

Exercise 1.—Learn to keep your head perfectly still for two or three minutes at a time. Sit upright in front of a mirror and keep your gaze fixed on any part of the head. Determine that you will not allow any movement of the head.

Exercise 2.—(a) Sit as before, in front of a mirror and keep your gaze fixed on the center of the chest. Keep perfectly still for at least two minutes. There should be no movement other than that attendant on the function of breathing. (b) Stand in the center of the room with your eyes closed and try to keep the body perfectly still. As a variation try to imagine you are standing on the brink of a precipice, and then check the tendency of the body to fall forward.   (c) Lie down on a bed, sofa, or couch, for two minutes and try to keep every muscle perfectly still.

Exercise 3.—(a) Hold either arm straight out from the body. Concentrate upon keeping the arm perfectly still for one or two minutes. (b) Stand on one leg, and extend the other leg about six to twelve inches from the body. Keep your gaze fixed on the boot of the foot extended, and try to avoid any movement for one or two minutes. Practice with each leg alternately.

(b) *The Facial Muscles.*—The facial muscles are a most important group to the student of self-consciousness. They control the movements of the eyes, lips, mouth, and are to be found in the brow, cheeks, and nose. They are, generally speaking, an index to the mind, for they express the transient play of the most subtle emotions, the basest passions, and the finer feelings. To the trained observer, they betray a man's real character and intelligence, and are also a valuable means of diagnosing various mental diseases.

(c) *How To Control The Facial Muscles.*—There are two ways in which to practice control over the facial muscles, viz., (1) To watch the play of these muscles in other people, and (2) to study them in ourselves with the aid of a mirror.

(1) In watching other people you are advised to watch carefully the movements of the LIPS AND MOUTH, for they are a great index to character. The tightly compressed lips are associated with precision and strength of will and purpose. The widely open mouth signifies astonishment and wonder, the partially open mouth indicates lack of precision, lack of purpose, and lack of ambition. When the corners of the mouth are drawn downwards, it signifies that a person is out of spirits.

The muscles of the EYE should have careful attention; they are fairly easy to read. We all know the sparkle of the eye of the person who is glad or full of joy, the fishy dead looking eye of the man who is in despair, the narrow glint of the man who is suspicious, the stern gaze of the man who is annoyed or angry, the shifty gaze of the man who is sly or treacherous, the fierce glare of the man filled with hate and fury, the downcast gaze of the man who is shy, timid, or bashful. The eyebrows should also be noted, for when they are oblique they denote deep dejection or anxiety. Note, too, the working of the muscles around the eyes when a person is in pain. Note, again, when a man or woman is sad or tired, the relaxed character of the muscles of the face as a whole; also, the slight tension of these muscles when a person is glad, and their strong contraction when under the influence of great anger.

The student of the facial muscles who habitually studies their working in other people will find that this practice tends to put him on his guard, and almost unconsciously he will seek to check the play of these muscles when such action is deemed necessary.

(2) After a certain amount of careful observation, as outlined above, you are advised to sit in front of a mirror for a few minutes each day, and to try to compose the muscles of the face as a whole. Keep the lips gently compressed, and gaze steadily at a point immediately between the eyes (*i.e.*, about the center of the root of the nose) and at the same time feel you are perfectly cool, calm, and self-possessed. After a few weeks' practice, as above, you will be able to control your facial muscles fairly well, in ordinary circumstances. To control these muscles in critical situations is possible only when one can control one's emotions—this I deal with in the next section.

I must warn you that *perfect* control of the facial muscles is not to be hoped for, since the facial muscles are not entirely under the control of the will. Some of their movements are involuntary, and are due to reflex action initiated by sensations in which consciousness plays no part. So far as this book is concerned these reflex movements are unimportant.

SECTION THIRTY-TWO.

HOW TO CONTROL YOUR EMOTIONS.

(a) *The Nature Of Emotion.*—An emotion may be described, in brief, as a tendency to feel, or more fully, as a mode of experience in which the feeling aspect is prominent. By feeling it will be understood that I refer to the mental shock in an emotion, and the visceral and bodily changes which always accompany it. While it is true that in emotion the feeling aspect is prominent, it should be noted that the feeling is entirely dependent on cognition through perception. Thus, to take the emotion of fear, for instance, unless we perceive that an object (*i.e.*, animal, person, or thing) is dangerous, or likely to bring us, or cause us, harm, the emotion of fear is not aroused.

The order of the events in an emotional state may, therefore, be summed up as follows: (1) The perception of some exciting fact, (2) bodily disturbance correlated with the mental shock, (3) the apprehension of the bodily disturbance, (4) an instinctive tendency to act (for every emotion has its correlate instinct).

Emotions are marked by two outstanding features (1) Their tendency to persist when once aroused, and (2) their tendency to attack anything which comes within their range. Thus under (1) if we feel angry with a person it is difficult to quell our anger; we require time to cool down. Under (2), when we are vexed, we are apt to vent our anger, not only on the person or thing that has caused our anger, but on anyone and anything.

(b) *How To Control An Emotion.*—There are two difficulties facing us when we attempt to control an emotion. We have to overcome the effects of the mental shock, and also the effect of the bodily disturbance, which manifests itself outwardly and inwardly. For the self-conscious person it is important that he should commence the control of an emotion by gaining a measure of control over the outward signs of the bodily disturbance.

Commence the control of the outward signs of an emotion by using *at once* your powers of inhibition to check the movements of the head, trunk, limbs, facial muscles, wherever any of these are involved. It may be that only the limbs, or perhaps only the facial muscles will be involved, but whatever the part may be, you must attempt *at once* to check the muscular movement by using your powers of inhibition; I have already laid down the way to train these powers.

You must next proceed to overcome the effects of the mental shock, for while this persists the inward bodily disturbance continues active, and this in its turn affects the full control of the outward signs of an emotion. Let us make this clear. If you have received a great fright, and have managed by inhibition to control, to a fair extent, the outward signs of your fright (the trembling limbs, facial movements, etc.), you still feel the effects of your fright in your mind and body—you are out of sorts, unsettled, not yourself. How are you to get rid of this disturbed feeling?

There are three main ways by which you can overcome the mental effects (and through this the bodily effects) of an emotion. (1) By simulation, (2) by analysis, (3) by thought-control. Let us look at these.

(1) To overcome the mental effect by simulation you must attempt to simulate the opposite of the emotion experienced, or you must simulate some emotion which is accompanied by mental and bodily disturbance of a more pleasant character than that experienced. Thus if you have been afraid you can simulate the emotion of exhilaration—the joyous, full-of-life feeling, which in turn arouses the instinct of assertiveness—the bold, not afraid-of-anything feeling. I shall show you the way to use simulation when I come to discuss suggestion. You will, also, grasp

its full significance when I take each type of self-consciousness, and consider the means of cure.

(2) When you analyze an emotion you rob it of a great deal of its power, for you should note that the tendency of emotion is to check the reasoning powers. Suppose you fear to do something, to speak at a public meeting, for instance. The emotion of fear at once tends to make you put your reason to one side and paint everything black: "I am sure to break down," "I am sure to make a fool of myself," etc., etc. When you come to analyze your fear, to look it squarely in the face, and ask the grounds of your fear, you can often see much that cheers you and encourages you to make the attempt to speak in public. Thus, you have a good grip of your subject, you have friends in the audience who wish you to do well, you are on an intellectual level with the majority of your audience, and so on.

(3) The employment of thought-control towards overcoming the mental shock in emotion is to strengthen the application of control through simulation. The main idea is to direct the mind into new channels of thought so as to soothe the mind and quiet the body. If you will follow the directions in the next section I can promise you good results.

In closing this section, I must impress upon you that it is not necessary to employ all the three ways of control indicated above, for the control of any particular emotion. *Experience, and your own judgment, will tell you which way is the most likely to secure the end you wish.*

SECTION THIRTY-THREE.

HOW TO CONTROL YOUR THOUGHTS.

"Thought-control" is such an important subject that a large volume could easily be devoted to it. As my objective is simply the control of thought in so far as self-consciousness is concerned, I need not go minutely into the matter

here. I shall give one or two general exercises, and you will be shown later how to adapt these to specific cases.

The beginning of all thought-control, as I have already stated, *is found in inhibition.* You cannot prevent thoughts from entering your mind, but you *can* prevent them from dwelling there. *The way to do this is through inhibition.*

Suppose, for instance, there comes into your mind the idea to commit some moral offense. If the idea be repellant, you have no difficulty in checking it. If, however, it be tempting and appeals to you your only safeguard is to check the idea *instantly.* You must on no account dwell upon it, or you may be lost, for the mind will at once proceed to form a train of thought that will widen out until it becomes more and more difficult for you to resist the appeal of the idea. Remember then, your safety lies in your getting away from the idea of the offense *at once.* Turn your mind into other channels. Think of something totally different or opposite in character to the idea that has entered your mind. Read a book, engage in some hobby, enter into conversation, if possible, or do some manual work. In a few minutes, you will find that the idea will gradually lose its power and the mind will proceed to form other associates.

Here are three exercises that will help you to gain a good measure of control over your thoughts. They bring into play your powers of inhibition and concentration. It should be noted that strong concentrative power is essential to the effective use of inhibition, as indeed to every form of control, mental and physical.

Exercise 1.—Practice diligently, for a few minutes each day, setting thoughts to one side as soon as they enter the mind. Do not allow them to form a train of thought.

Exercise 2.—Concentrate your mind on one idea to the exclusion of every other idea. Take the word control, for instance. Concentrate solely on the word, not on what it represents. Repeat to yourself: "I am thinking of the word control, not of anything else." Take a different word each day, and keep your mind on it for one minute at a time.

Exercise 3.—Place your finger on any part of your body, and concentrate upon the sensation the touch gives rise to. Do not allow your mind to stray to other ideas; keep it solely on the touch sensation.

SECTION THIRTY-FOUR.

THE THIRD STAGE.

The third stage in the path of control is of extreme importance. *Here stands the guide-post that points the way to the cure of every type of self-consciousness.* This guide-post is named *"Suggestion."* You are earnestly advised to get a thorough grasp of the nature and use of suggestion, for it is of fundamental importance.

(*a*) *The Nature Of Suggestion.*—You are suffering from some complaint. You have tried this doctor and that doctor but have failed to get relief. One day you read an advertisement in a newspaper that exactly describes your complaint and then proceeds to tell you where, and at what price, you can secure the means of cure. The advertisement is a suggestion to you whether you buy the cure or not. *Its power over you is determined by the appeal it makes to you.*

Suggestion surrounds us on every side; no man or woman escapes its influence. It attacks us from within and without at every hour of the day. We all act on suggestions that appeal to us. Every book, newspaper, or magazine, every person we see or with whom we have converse, everything we look at, everything we hear, everything we touch, smell, or taste, all send out suggestions; some feeble, others so powerful that we obey them at once. The greater part of what we term our thinking is not thinking at all—*a suggestion comes and we act upon it.*

(*b*) *The Mechanism Of Suggestion.*—Whenever an idea

or image enters consciousness it tends naturally to result in movement. To put this technically: ideal states tend to be followed by motor states. If the idea be feeble, and does not excite interest, it rapidly gives way to other ideas. If it is a strong idea attention is aroused, and we act on the idea or reject it. Every idea that enters consciousness has numerous associates; some of these are in harmony with the idea, and others are antagonistic to it. In normal circumstances, every idea, when attention is paid to it, is subject to the conscious direction of the will. The attention in suggestion differs from ordinary attention for it is attended by no conscious direction of the will.

The characteristic of a suggestion-idea, if I may so term it, is that it generally makes its entrance into consciousness with a startling abruptness. At once all ideas not in harmony with the suggestion are inhibited; all sensory and motor paths except those in agreement with the suggested idea are blocked, hence the simplification of the motor discharge from the suggested idea. This is bound to follow unless a more powerful suggestion enters consciousness and in turn inhibits the former suggestion.

I must ask the reader, therefore, to keep in mind the difference between a suggestion-idea and any other idea, viz., its power to shut out every other idea of an opposite or interfering character. The man who is under the spell of a suggestion-idea is, for the time being, *hypnotized by the idea, forced to attend to it and to carry out its demands.*

(c) *The Power Of Suggestion.*—The power of suggestion varies; we are all more suggestible at certain times than at other times. When we are tired, or under the influence of emotion, drugs, intoxicants, our suggestibility is increased. Any weakening of the critical powers of judgment clears the path for suggestion.

Suggestion works in a very subtle way: anything can be the exciting cause. We all know how quickly it can act; as an example take the following: You awake in the middle of the night and feel you would like a drink of water. You have no strong desire for a drink, all you want is a mouthful, or say, half-a-tumbler of water. When you remember that there is no water in the room, *at once* the suggestion comes: "I want a drink badly; I want a big drink; I'm dying for a drink." In this way the suggestion grows more and more powerful, until your thirst becomes intolerable, and forces you, perhaps, to go in search of water.

As an example of the subtle, stealthy approach of suggestion the following will suffice:—

A man accustomed to drink several glasses of ale every night without any signs of intoxication was invited by the landlord of a public-house, to which he went occasionally, to try a glass of a famous strong ale which the landlord had recently bought. While the man was supping the ale the landlord told him it was *so* strong that it would knock anyone over. "Why, just last night," said he, "a big strong fellow came in and had *one* glass, and it took him all his time to get out of the door." The man, who had had already two or three glasses of ordinary ale was so strongly impressed by the landlord's talk, that although he had supped only a small quantity of the ale, he began to feel all the symptoms of intoxication and had to hurry home.

(Note the preparation for the suggestion given by the landlord at the words *"so strong,"* and the entrance of the suggestion at the words *"one glass."*)

(d) *Semi-Suggestion In Everyday Life.*—Semi-suggestion is very common in our everyday life, and is ruled by our desires or wishes. Thus, if the sky is cloudy and we have a strong desire to go somewhere, we say to ourselves: "I don't think it will rain to-day." With a similar cloudy sky and a weak desire to go out we say, "I won't go out just now; I'm certain there will be a deluge soon." Again, at one time a pain in a particular part of the body is dismissed by us as not worth worrying about; at another time a somewhat similar pain in the same part of the body is looked upon as the breaking-up of our constitution.

Semi-suggestion will sometimes develop into real suggestion but generally it has not the force of suggestion proper; it is a conflict of ideas and sometimes it is a fairly lengthy process before action results. You will find it interesting and profitable to review your actions at the close of the day, and see to what extent they have been influenced by semi-suggestion.

(e) *Auto-Suggestion.*—Auto-suggestion, as the name implies, is suggestion made to the self, *i.e.*, suggestions made to a person by himself, hence another name for it is self-suggestion.

There are two forms of auto-suggestion, the unconscious form and the conscious form. Under the former a person is unaware that he is using suggestion; under the latter he is perfectly aware that he is using suggestion. It is because of this unawareness, and also on account of its being more of the nature of suggestion proper, that the unconscious form of auto-suggestion has a much greater influence upon our lives. For one person who uses auto-suggestion consciously there are thousands that use it unconsciously.

Auto-suggestion in the unconscious form represents the talking and communing with ourselves which forms the springs of conduct and action; we are what our auto-suggestions have made us. A few examples will illustrate this. Some men are always bewailing their luck; others are convinced that they were born under a lucky star. Some men constantly dread failure; others as confidently expect success. Some men are always concerned about their health, others never give it a thought—they feel full of health and strength. These states of mind, or mental attitudes towards life, in all these classes of men, are the results of a long series of auto-suggestions.

We are now in a position to distinguish between suggestion proper and the unconscious form of auto-suggestion.

The former always works quickly; sometimes there is a slight preparatory stage, but the real attack is always characterized by an abruptness of entry. In the unconscious form of auto-suggestion there is no abruptness of entry. The suggestions represent a long series of repetitions which through the law of habit grow in strength until they become rooted in the personality. As a result of this process of repetition, conscious direction of the will plays little or no part, hence in time these auto-suggestions function in the same manner as real suggestions.

The conscious form of auto-suggestion is familiar to many people through their reading of new-thought literature, and also to another section of the public from its use in *psycho-therapeutic* treatment. It works on the same lines as the unconscious form of auto-suggestion, viz., by repetitions, but with this difference; the repetitions are always under the conscious direction of the will, hence the results are not so true and sure (with most people) as in the unconscious form of auto-suggestion. Let me illustrate this.

A person, using the conscious form of auto-suggestion, says: "I am strong," "I am in perfect health," "I feel fit for anything." He uses his will to emphasize this, to spur himself on. If the suggestions were real, *i.e.*, the result of outside stimuli, all ideas antagonistic to his statements would be inhibited, but in conscious auto-suggestion, this is not so. Many *know* they are not strong, or in perfect health, hence there is a conflict of ideas, with the result that in the majority of cases their suggestions fail—their strength and health remain as before. In the unconscious form of auto-suggestion, the conscious will is absent, and with the constant repetitions the body falls in line with the thought.

(*f*) *How To Use Auto-Suggestion Consciously.*—As I have indicated above, the great difficulty is using auto-suggestion consciously is the conflict of ideas. This difficulty can be attacked in four ways, viz., by (1) Limitation, (2) simulation, (3) inhibition, (4) concentration.

Suppose, for instance, you wish to improve your health by conscious auto-suggestion. If your health is poor it will be apparent to you that it is absurd to use the auto-suggestion—"I am in perfect health." To say this is at once to raise a conflict of ideas. You know you are *not* in perfect health, indeed you are very far from it. It is better, therefore, to limit your auto-suggestion within reasonable bounds and say: "I am well to-day." You must next simulate what you conceive to be a state of "wellness." You must try to picture this state of health in your mind, and then try to give it bodily expression. You will simulate a pleased expression, a happy expression, a joyous expression, in your face. You will walk briskly, meet your friends with a smile, in short, you will try to act exactly as a person who feels well would act.

So far you will not find the above program difficult, but after an hour or so, perhaps less, a slight pain, a feeling of fatigue, or any feeling common to your ordinary state of health will manifest itself, and then doubts will arise in your mind as to the worth of auto-suggestion. Now is the time to employ inhibition. You must check these thoughts *at once,* and keep up simulation. It is not easy to do, especially when alone, but constant practice will make it easier. It is here that concentration comes in. You must keep your aim ever before you—better health, this state of "wellness" which you wish to secure to yourself. Keep your mind concentrated on the statement "I am well to-day." Keep simulating the *feeling* of wellness, and instantly inhibit anything that tends to make you doubt the efficacy of the auto-suggestion.

I cannot impress upon you too strongly the necessity for limitation in auto-suggestion; it is the safest way to lessen the conflict of ideas. Try to keep your auto-suggestion in line with your life and environment, and proceed by easy stages to higher things. Thus, when you are able to simulate successfully the state of wellness, you can go a step further and say: "My health is growing better every day," next, "I am full of life and vim," and so on until you can use the auto-suggestion "I am in perfect health." Practice on these lines with all your auto-suggestions, and back them up with simulation, inhibition, and concentration, and I can promise you success to your efforts.

There is another method of using auto-suggestion consciously, which some people have found useful, viz., by what is sometimes termed self-treatment. You lie down on a couch or sofa, with muscles relaxed, and fix your gaze on some bright object, such as an electric light, gas light, or lamp. When a sense of drowsiness is felt, you make your auto-suggestion. A variation of this method is to make your auto-suggestion immediately on awakening in the morning, or at night just at the point of falling asleep. Personally, I have found the method of limitation, simulation, inhibition and concentration to give the best results.

SECTION THIRTY-FIVE.

THE FOURTH STAGE.

You are now prepared to enter the *Fourth Stage* of the path of control so as to secure to yourself the weapons with which to fight fear, viz., *self-reliance, self-confidence, calmness* and *self-possession*.

The chief means to use to secure these weapons must be through auto-suggestion, *i.e.*, by affirmations made to yourself. And here it is necessary to put you on your guard so that you may use auto-suggestion effectively. In making affirmations never use the negative form. Thus, suppose a self-conscious person were to say: "I shall not be self-conscious any more," such a form of affirmation would be foolish, for through the law of habit an affirmation of this kind tends to keep the thought of his self-consciousness ever in mind. For remember, the word self-conscious is associated in his mind with so much of the fear and mistrust element that, at any moment, when he uses the affirmation, the word self-conscious may bring with it, through the law of association of ideas, thoughts of fear or self-mistrust, and at a critical moment wreck his self-control.

(a) *How To Gain Self-Reliance.*—Let us first try to grasp what self-reliance means. The word really is a compound of re (meaning "back") and ly or lie (meaning "to rest"). To rely on anything meant originally to rest by lying back on the thing, hence the word reliance came to signify dependence on some thing, or object; by a natural extension the word was applied to persons, signifying dependence on others. Opposed to this came the word self-reliance, signifying dependence on one's self, on one's own powers and abilities.

How is a man to proceed who desires to become self-reliant? The answer is simple—he must give up the practice of leaning on others. He must think things out for himself, he must try to form his own opinions on all kinds of things, he must learn to act on his own initiative. Instead of waiting for others to come to his aid, he must strike out for himeslf. He must constantly spur himself on with auto-suggestion. Thus he will say: "I am resolved to think this thing out for myself," "I *will* find the way to do this thing," "I have every faith in my own abilities." He must carry the spirit of these affirmations into everything he does, everything he attempts.

It will assist you greatly in seeking to cultivate self-reliance if you will carefully think out to what extent you really rely on others in your daily life. Ask yourself to what extent you rely on others in forming your opinions—do you rely on a particular book, magazine or newspaper? If so, do a little hard thinking instead; use your reasoning powers and see where they lead you. In business, do you rely on some particular person to help you in a difficulty? If so, try to solve your difficulties yourself. Exert yourself, think for yourself, act for yourself, and then you will naturally come to rely on yourself; you will be self-reliant.

(g) *How To Gain Self-Confidence.*—The man who has learned to rely on himself will find that he has taken the first step towards gaining self-confidence.

Self-confidence means having confidence in one's ability to do things, and as a man begins to rely on himself and finds that he *can* do things, he gains confidence in his power to do certain things. As this power grows (as it will in proportion as a man relies on himself) he will attack new things with a faith in his power to conquer the new thing.

There is a great difference between self-confidence which has been acquired, and the confidence of a certain type of man whom we popularly term the confident man. The latter is so confident of his power to do things that he often fails through lack of caution and for want of using all the means necessary to success. The man who has *acquired* self-confidence has knowledge of himself; he knows what he can do, and he bases everything upon this self-knowledge. He plans out his campaign, leaves nothing to chance, and makes sure he has a thorough grasp of the situation. He constantly spurs himself on by auto-suggestion, "I am confident I can do this," "I have every confidence in my power to do this, to carry this through."

If you want to gain self-confidence you must rely on yourself; take courage from your victories, and constantly use auto-suggestion to help you in new ventures. In this way self-confidence, confidence in your own abilities, will grow more and more, and help you to succeed in whatever you undertake.

(c) *How To Gain Calmness.*—A calm man is one who is able to control his feelings. The signs of calmness are shown in the face by a gentle relaxation of the muscles suggestive of repose and latent power. A calm man, therefore, always carries with him a sense of dignity and power, in the eyes of other people. The signs of calmness in the body are absence of jerkiness of motion or nervous tension; the muscles of the head, trunk, and limbs all appear to be thoroughly under control.

To gain calmness, you are advised to gain control over the facial muscles, and also control over the muscles of the head, trunk and limbs. You must also seek to gain control over your emotions, and take every opportunity to strengthen your powers of inhibition, and to practice control over your thoughts. In times of stress you must use auto-suggestion by affirming calmness. ''I am calm; nothing can disturb my calmness.'' Close your eyes while you say this, and try to feel an inner calmness—this is important. This inner calmness will manifest itself according to your power of concentration. Repeat your affirmation of calmness when anything tends to ruffle you. Try to carry this spirit of calmness into your daily life. Gradually there will come the power to look at everything in a cool, calm, collected state of mind. You will find that in the midst of excitement and bustle you can always call upon this spirit of calmness, and that it will protect you, like a shield, from the disturbing influences surrounding you.

(d) *How To Gain Self-Possession.*—Self-possession involves complete control over one's self, *i.e.*, control over our physical and mental powers at any time, but more especially when danger is apprehended, or when a sudden crisis presents itself.

To be self-possessed a man must have self-reliance, self-confidence, and the calm attitude of mind—these we have already discussed. He must have in addition to the above the power of thinking quickly and acting quickly, and all that we understand by presence of mind.

To acquire the power of thinking quickly and acting quickly, *i.e.*, the power of quick decision, you must begin with the little things of life. If you seek to quicken your thinking power, you must check yourself in your general reading and in your studies; you must pull up suddenly and ask yourself if you understand what you have just read. You must answer quickly, and afterwards, when time permits, you must go closely into the matter and try to determine what errors of reasoning or judgment you have made. In business, or in professional life, when faced with alternatives, you must try to decide quickly so as to act one way or the other.

I hope it will be clear to you what I am seeking to inculcate, viz., the practice of making up your mind instantly, so as to be ready to act in critical moments. Unless you practice quick decision in the minor matters of life, you cannot hope to face difficult situations with success. You will, of course, make mistakes, but if you review the matter afterwards you will discover your weak points and be on your guard another time. Never mind your mistakes; accept them as part of the discipline you are undergoing. As you gain the power to act quickly you are preparing yourself for occasions when quick decision is vital.

I earnestly advise every self-conscious person to give careful attention to this section; self-possession is vital to him, and will help him enormously in grappling with his self-consciousness.

CHAPTER VI.

THE FEAR OF A CROWD.

SECTION THIRTY-SIX.

THE CURE OF FEARS THAT ATTACK THE SELF-CONSCIOUS.

Before I proceed to discuss the means of cure of each particular fear included in this section, a few words of explanation are necessary.

From my analysis of the various forms of fear, it will be apparent to you that none of these forms exists in a pure state; each is a complex, *i.e.*, each type of fear is closely related to some other type of fear, and also involves some of the factors discussed under "SECONDARY CAUSES OF SELF-CONSCIOUSNESS" and "SPECIAL CAUSES OF SELF-CON-SCIOUSNESS," Thus, for instance, the fear of self has a close relationship to the fear of failure, fear of criticism, fear of the unexpected; also with timidity, shyness, ridicule, nervousness.

In treating the cure of each type of fear, I shall deal with the broad features or outstanding characteristics of each type, and leave you yourself to link up the minor features. Thus, if you are conscious that timidity plays an important rôle in your fear of yourself, after reading my instructions for the cure of the fear of self, you will then turn to the section treating of THE CURE OF TIMIDITY, and so link up the two sections.

You are advised to read in PART TWO the analysis of each type of fear in conjunction with the cure of each type, so as to get a good grasp of the situation.

SECTION THIRTY-SEVEN.

HOW TO CURE THE FEAR OF SELF.

We found the signs of the fear of self to be (1) Depreciation of self, and (2) underestimating one's abilities. If you have the fear of self, you will recognize it by these signs in yourself. Now, if by some magic aid you could make these signs disappear in an instant, you would find their place taken by a new sign symptomatic of a brighter state, viz., belief in self. All your old habits of running yourself down and cherishing a poor opinion of your abilities would be gone, and in place of them would be a strong belief in yourself, and in your power to do whatever task was set before you. Do you grasp my meaning? *The cure of the fear of self must proceed on the lines of belief of self.* You must learn to believe in yourself, and then your fear of yourself will disappear.

Every man believes in himself to *some* extent; he knows he *can* do certain things. He knows that he can do his daily work sufficiently well to pass muster or to preserve his employment. He knows that he can read certain books with a full understanding of what he reads. He knows that he can play certain games as well as the average player. He knows that he can sing, or play an instrument well enough to give satisfaction to his home circle or to a few intimate friends. He knows that he can eat and drink certain foods and liquids without any fear of consequences. He knows that among certain people he has not the slightest fear. I think, therefore, it will be fairly clear that every man does believe in himself in some degree. The weakening of his belief comes in only when there is any departure from the normal, when he is called upon to do something unusual. In other words, ask a man to come out of his rut, and at once his fear of self tends to appear.

I suggest that the man who desires to grow belief in self should proceed as follows: He should sit down quietly and review the things he *can* do. Let him make a list of these things, so that there may be no mistake about it. He should then, with his list in front of him, reason with himself as follows: "I can do all these things; I know I can. I can do them whenever it is required of me." Now what has this man done? He has laid the foundation upon which to build a fuller belief in self—he has made a start towards a better state of things. He begins to realize that he *does* believe in himself; he begins to realize the relationship of belief in self to knowledge of self. *When a man reaches this stage he is in a position to grasp the significance of the following rules:*

RULE 1.—Check (through inhibition) any thought tending to depreciation of self.

RULE 2.—Check any and every tendency to underestimate your abilities. Refuse to dwell on such thoughts—in this way they lose their power over you.

RULE 3.—Encourage in every way belief in yourself—use auto-suggestion constantly to this end.

The man who is afflicted with the fear of self must make up his mind to employ the above rules constantly in his daily life; their application will not be difficult unless some sudden call is made on his belief. Suppose, for instance, you have applied these rules, and met with a fair measure of success, and then one day you are offered an important position. You may find it difficult now to keep back doubts as to your ability to fill such a position. You should remember this, however: the person who offers you the position must have *some* faith in your ability to occupy the position, or he would certainly not offer it to you. I ask you to lay stress upon this point of view. Say to yourself, "It is quite evident that the man who has offered me this position regards me as capable of filling it. I shall, therefore, accept it, and do my utmost to give satisfaction."

Try to look upon an invitation from others asking you to accept responsibility or to perform some service for them as a proof of their belief in you, and in your ability to do what they require of you. These people often know more about you than you do yourself; they have watched you quietly, and have summed you up, and in the great majority of cases their estimate of you is correct. There is another way to look at this; where you feel that a person has a good opinion of you, naturally you strive to do all you can to merit that opinion, hence you call up reserve powers of energy, and do your utmost to please that person.

As you learn to believe in yourself, you will find that your belief in self will grow stronger and stronger after each test or trial, until it becomes a driving force in your life. You will enjoy new tests of strength, for you will feel convinced that you will come out of them all right, and thus add to your belief in self. One of the most delightful feelings a man can have, is this growing belief in self, and it will be yours if you will follow the lines I have laid herein. To hasten the process, sedulously cultivate your powers of self-reliance and self-confidence, for in this way you will gain knowledge of yourself, and the more you grow in this knowledge, the greater will be your power to do what you undertake to do.

SECTION THIRTY-EIGHT.

HOW TO CURE THE FEAR OF CROWDS.

In my analysis of this fear I divided it into two forms —*the active form and the passive form.* The active form does not really come within the scope of this book. I may say, however, that anyone who carries out the instructions given in the "PRELIMINARY TRAINING FOR THE CURE OF SELF-CONSCIOUSNESS" will equip himself well.

The passive form of this fear is that which specially concerns the self-conscious person. I have instanced several situations in which this form is liable to appear. Thus, when entering a public-meeting, church, concert-hall, large store; entering a train, motor-bus, steamer, etc. All these situations may be said to be fundamentally one. In each case you have a number of people looking at you, watching your movements, taking stock of everything about you, and at the same time smiling and laughing at your discomfiture. To make the matter quite clear I shall select one of these situations and examine it thoroughly.

A young man enters a public conveyance—it does not matter whether it is a train, motor-bus, or electric-car. As he enters he meets the gaze of every occupant of the conveyance. If he is troubled with self-consciousness, instantly there comes over him the fear of the crowd. He is conscious that all these people are looking at him, and he is sure that they are examining every little thing about him with the object of making fun of him. Those who are smiling or laughing are smiling or laughing at him. As a result of such thoughts he often does foolish things, or looks foolish, and in this way excites ridicule.

Now what is the mental attitude of the crowd when they see a stranger enter a public conveyance? It is simply one of curiosity—idle curiosity. They do not care a rap who he is or what he looks like—they would give a dog or cat equal attention, perhaps more. In a few seconds they have forgotten the "extraordinary" fact that he has entered; he has now become one of the company, and if he conducts himself properly no one will give another thought to him. As soon as you grasp the full significance of the attitude of the crowd you will find it very comforting. I advise you to keep it in mind whenever you are in the presence of the crowd, and you will find that the fear of the crowd will have little power over you.

(a) SPECIAL RULES TO CURE THE FEAR OF THE CROWD.

RULE 1.—On entering a public conveyance, public-meeting, etc., keep in mind this central fact—the attitude of the crowd towards you is simply one of idle curiosity.

RULE 2.—As you proceed to your seat, control your facial

muscles and switch your mind away from thoughts of the crowd.

RULE 3.—When you are settled in your seat look unobtrusively at ONE person, avoiding his eyes. Note how he is dressed, and try to sum up what kind of a person he is. After a minute or so shift your gaze and look around you. The short rest will have given you time to compose yourself and you will find you can look about without any sense of discomfort.

RULE 4.—If you see people laughing and talking do not be so silly as to imagine they are laughing or talking about you; they are probably (very probably) never wasting a thought on you. Turn your mind away from such foolish fancies, and direct your thoughts into some more profitable channel and your foolish fears will soon cease to trouble you.

There is one point in connection with the fear of the crowd to which it is necessary to draw attention, and that is the common act of walking. It is a simple act to walk across the floor of an empty room, or across the stage of an empty theatre, or concert-hall; it is *not* easy to walk across these spaces when there is a number of people watching you. Why? *Simply because then you begin to pay attention to HOW you walk with the result that the automaticity of your steps is interfered with.* To walk across a room, stage, etc., in a natural manner you must fix your mind on what you are going to do, and then your walk will appear natural.

(b) ADOLESCENTS AND THE FEAR OF THE CROWD.

All I have said above is specially important in the case of adolescents. There are one or two points, however, which will require consideration.

Adolescents are specially liable to fear of the crowd when the crowd is composed of (1) Members of opposite sex—thus boys are specially liable to this fear in the presence of girls, and *vice versa*—and, (2) when in the presence of adults, especially those of grave demeanor. Now there is only one method of cure in such cases and it will not be so difficult as it appears if a boy or girl will carry out the instructions I have already given. The adolescent must never shrink from encounters with these two special forms of the fear of the crowd. In the case of a boy, he must not mind the initial confusion of mind when in the presence of girls, or in the presence of adults; he must persevere, bearing in mind that only by resolute attack will he gain control over himself. Here as in everything else, the first steps are the most difficult, but where the attack is resolute he will soon note a great difference in himself. After every attempt he will be stronger and better able to control the mental confusion. He will be helped and comforted in his fight if he constantly bears in mind that *success is certain* if he keeps on with his efforts and never minds a failure now and again.

A girl must submit to the same discipline as a boy, but in her case special care will have to be taken that her fight is waged with strict attention to decorum.

SECTION THIRTY-NINE.

HOW TO CURE THE FEAR OF AUDIENCES.

I must point out at once that, strictly speaking, it is not possible to lay down rules for the *absolute* cure of fear of audiences. The roots of this fear are strong and deep, and you *must control* it so that you may be able to face an audience with some degree of comfort.

Every man, even the most hardened, who faces an audience, is conscious of a feeling of strain, uneasiness, or more or less nervous excitement. With the practiced speaker or performer this sense of strain, uneasiness, or nervous excitement, rapidly disappears as he warms to his work. With many of these people it is incorrect to say that they fear the audience; the bodily or mental signs of strain or nervous excitement are more of the nature of reflex action. Just as you cannot help blinking when anyone aims a blow at your eye, even when you know there is no intention of hitting you, so when you come before an audience you cannot help feeling for the moment a certain sense of strain, etc. If you allow this state of feeling to be of the nature of reflex action, and not actual fear, then I may with confidence lay down rules or give guidance to overcome the fear of an audience.

You must distinguish two forms of this fear: (1) Fear prior to coming before the audience, and (2) fear when actually before the audience.

To cure fear prior to coming before an audience, you must use the agent that causes the fear. You found this (*Section 10*) to be prefunctioning. Prior to coming before the audience you visualize the scene and all that you imagine will take place, with the result that when the time comes for facing the audience your nerve is gone, and either you fail to put in an appearance, or fail to do justice to yourself. Now this prefunctioning, which has worked the evil, is capable of accomplishing quite an opposite result. It should be employed as follows:—

Sit down or lie down with eyes closed and try to visualize the scene of your engagement. Imagine you see the audience. Imagine you see the platform or stage and yourself looking at the sea of faces in front of you, but with no distress of mind or body. Again, imagine you see yourself coming on the platform in a cool, quiet, collected manner, and going to work in a spirit of confidence. Try to visualize the scene of your successful finish, and the applause of the audience when you retire. In all your prefunctioning aim at success throughout; never allow your mind to dwell for a moment on the possibility of failure. As soon as you complete the visualization of your successful finish, stop the prefunctioning, and get up and engage in something that will take your mind away from your engagement. Refuse to dwell on it, and use all your powers of inhibition to this end. This checking of the train of thought is all-important for the success of your prefunctioning. One word more: If the thought of your engagement enters your mind during the day, refuse to allow it to form a train of thought; turn the mind at once into some other channel.

We have now to consider the second form of the fear of audiences, viz., fear when actually before the audience. You saw that this also may be of two kinds: (1) The fear which comes from a sudden call to appear before an audience, and (2) the fear which attacks one when actually before an audience.

The fear due to a sudden call need not detain us long. Such an invitation should not be accepted except by those accustomed to appear in public; success on the part of a novice cannot be looked for in the great majority of cases. The fear of the sudden call is strictly not so much fear of the audience as fear due to a sense of being unprepared. Such a fear is quite natural, and a man is wise to pay heed to it, and gently and politely to refuse the call unless he can see a glimmer of success likely to attend his efforts.

In dealing with the fear that attacks one when actually before an audience, you must distinguish between the fear of a man accustomed to appear before the public and the fear of the novice.

I stated in my analysis of the fear of audiences that the greatest artistes and the greatest orators were not exempt from this fear. The fear of these people has a dual aspect. It is due partly to what is termed a state of feeling of the nature of reflex action, and also to a feeling of responsibility. A great pianist, for instance, knows that he has a great reputation to sustain. His audience is sympathetic, and looks forward with pleasure to his performance, but allowing for all this, the great pianist is aware of another thing, a most important thing—his audience is also a critical audience. If he is playing a great work, he knows there will be a certain number of people in his audience who will know every note of the work and how it should be played. It is this knowledge that constitutes his real fear, for he knows that a finished performance is expected of him. He feels, therefore, that his artistic success trembles in the balance, and he is anxious both on account of that success and on account of his art. Similarly, a great orator knows that much is expected of him. He knows that oratory is an art, and must be used with art. He knows, also, that each audience represents a different problem, a different call upon his art, hence his fear that he may fail to do justice to his task.

Every man who has done good work before the public has had to pay the price of his success in his fear of the audience, and the remarkable thing about it is that if he were to lose this thrill of fear, he would lose also the greater part of his power. For the fear of the audience is really a blessing in disguise, strange as this may seem. It is a constant spur to a man to try to do his best on every occasion. This is what the great preacher meant to whom I referred (*Section* 10), when he said to the young clergyman who was anxious to get rid of the fear of the audience: "God help you if it were possible, for that same moment you would be lost." If a great artiste, orator,* preacher, or anyone who wishes to do well in public will only recognize that his fear of the crowd is a stimulus, a call to battle, a spur to put forth his best efforts, he will not wish to be rid of his fear. When he feels it, he will welcome it as an aid, and not regard it in the light of a deterrent. Previous encounters will remind him that the

---

* My latest book, "THE MASTER KEY," gives full instruction to *Public Speakers* and those who wish to control an audience. Published and sold only by MESSRS. DE LAURENCE, SCOTT & Co., Chicago, Ill., U. S. A.

fear thrill is only momentary, and will surely disappear as he rises to the stimulus. With every recurrence of his fear as he continues to come before the public, will come the memory of his past achievements, and past successes, and he will enter upon his new task with the spirit and confidence of one who goes on to victory.

I will now turn to the case of the novice with his reputation still to make. If he will ponder over what I have just said his fear of the fear of the audience will be on a different footing. He will not desire to be rid of the fear of the audience, for he will recognize that it is necessary if he aims at success before the public. As soon as he learns to look upon it as a spur and a stimulus he will cease to look upon it as an evil and a stumbling-block. The following rules should be strictly attended to by the novice.

RULE 1.—Never attempt anything in public without THOROUGH preparation for the part you seek to play.

RULE 2.—Never attempt anything in public which you cannot perform with the utmost facility in the privacy of your own home.

RULE 3.—Never attempt to pose in public; keep your thoughts centered on what you are going to do and then your pose will be natural, and will take care of itself.

RULE 4.—Remember that every audience is highly imitative and sensitive to impressions. If you appear nervous you make your audience nervous on your account. If you appear to be confident of your ability to do what you have come prepared to do your audience will be easy in mind. If you come on looking glum your audience will look glum. If you come on looking pleasant and good-humored your audience will catch your spirit and mood.

RULE 5.—Do not give your audience the feeling that you are rushing your work or you will make your audience restless. If you are a speaker speak slowly rather than quickly, with deliberation, and distinct articulation. Your audience will then give you better attention and you will not be so liable to danger from stage-fright.

RULE 6.—Never attempt a big part in public until you have succeeded in little parts. You can grow in ease and confidence only by graduating from small beginnings.

SECTION FORTY.

HOW TO CONTROL THE FEAR OF STAGE-FRIGHT.

You will note from the heading of this section that I do not purpose giving instructions for the *cure* of stage-fright. I have a reason for this. Stage-fright is a sudden fear, and may arise from so many causes which it is impossible to foresee that it would be folly to attempt its cure. All I can do is to lay down rules for the control of stage-fright when it makes its appearance. Let us look at two cases of the fear of stage-fright so that we may deduce therefrom guiding principles for the control of this fear.

A violinist is playing a concerto before a brilliant audience, and has a first-class orchestra playing the accompaniment. In a few minutes he knows he will have to play an elaborate and difficult *cadenza,* when, of course, the orchestral parts will be tacit. This *cadenza* has taken him weeks or perhaps months of hard practice to bring to perfection. Now there is always in the background of his consciousness a knowledge of the extreme difficulty of this *cadenza,* and on the present occasion there comes to him the thought: "Shall I be able to play it now?" He cannot account for the entrance of this thought, and instantly the fear of stage-fright makes its appearance. He knows that every violinist in the orchestra is on the look-out for the *cadenza*—perhaps many of them have struggled with it at home, and have always failed to be satisfied with their efforts, and hence are keen to see how he will tackle certain parts where they have always come to grief. He knows, too, that his audience will give special attention to the *cadenza,* for there will not be the sound of the other instruments to distract their attention. Now that stage-fright has made its attack, one of two things will happen: either he will break down, and he will be unable to play the *cadenza,* or he will manage to struggle through it in a way that will not be likely to enhance his reputation.

We will now look at our second case of the fear of stage-fright.

A well-known cabinet minister is in the middle of an impassioned speech, when suddenly he realizes that he has lost the thread of his discourse. With the realization of his loss he falls a victim to stage-fright. Either his speech ends in a sudden collapse, or he makes a tame finish.

A very slight examination of these two cases reveals a fundamental identity. In the first case the fear arises through doubt of his ability to perform a difficult task. In the second case the fear arises from a feeling of helplessness to proceed. Both the doubting and the helplessness rapidly lead to the fear of failure, and once this appears anything may happen. The fear of failure is the common fear in both these cases. If it is partially effective, we have in the case of the musician the tendency to speed up, to get through the work as quickly as possible; and in the case of the speakers we have either the same hurrying up tendency, or a slight paralysis of the motor centers of speech, bringing hesitation and confusion of thought. If the failure is fully effective, we have in both cases paralysis of movement and total break-down. The following rules for the control of stage-fright will be found effective. They follow naturally from my treatment of the subject.

RULE 1.—Make it a constant practice, no matter how wide your experience before the public may be, never to come before an audience without preparing yourself by auto-suggestion. Say to yourself, with deep feeling and conviction: "I shall do well to-night; I shall have a big success; everything will go without a hitch." Make suggestions like these and go before your public filled with their spirit of conviction, and by so doing you will minimize greatly the fear of stage-fright.

RULE 2.—If before going on to the platform you are conscious that your audience is a difficult one to satisfy, do not DWELL on this thought. Resolve to do your best, and use auto-suggestion to aid you in this.

RULE 3.—When doubts as to your ability to carry out your work before an audience enter your mind, you must check them INSTANTLY. Unless you check such thoughts at once they will spread with extreme rapidity until you will be powerless to stop their course.

RULE 4.—If your stage-fright is due to a sudden failure of memory, do not allow your audience to see that you are worried or ill at ease. Crave their indulgence in a pleasant manner. Tell them how you are situated, and in the great majority of cases you may rest assured you will have their sympathy, and you need not feel you have disgraced yourself or hurt your reputation.

RULE 5.—The same tactics should be employed if your failure to proceed is due to ill-health. Tell your audience you cannot go on; tell them you do not feel well enough. No audience will refuse its sympathy in such circumstances.

In closing this section I must ask you to remember the distinction between stage-fright and fear of an audience. It is common for people to say: "As soon as I set foot on the platform, I got an attack of stage-fright." As I have already said, such an experience is not stage-fright, but engaged rather the fear of an audience.

SECTION FORTY-ONE.

HOW TO CURE THE FEAR OF FAILURE.

In laying down rules for the cure of the fear of failure, I have to take into consideration its two forms, viz., (1) The form which acts as a check against initiative and enterprise, and (2) the form which attacks the man actively in various spheres of work.

I said (*Section* 12) that the first form was more common than the second form, and more difficult to cure. The reason why it is more difficult to cure is easy to grasp; it is a fixed habit of mind, and rules, in many cases, with the force of an obsession. For years these people have said: "I dare not risk a change. I'm afraid to go into a new line of business. I'm afraid to take a new part, afraid to venture into that scheme. I should be sure to fail," and so on.

Now, to alter or root up fixed habits of mind is not an easy task, but it *can* be done if a man will have the necessary pluck and perseverance. I ask people of this class to carry out the following rules, for I can guarantee their effectiveness:

RULE 1.—Put into practice at once the instructions given in "Preliminary Training for the Cure of Self-Consciousness," especially *Section* 35, (*a*) (*b*).

RULE 2.—Cultivate ambition by reading the lives of great men, especially those in your own sphere of work or that sphere to which your inclinations turn. The handicaps under which men have worked before they achieved success should shame you into activity and enterprise.

RULE 3.—Cease thinking and speaking of failure and have nothing to do with failures (men or women) until you are strong enough to do missionary work among them. Whenever failure-thoughts enter your mind inhibit them INSTANTLY.

RULE 4.—Never shirk a task because it is out of your usual routine. Have a shot at it. If you do not succeed on every occasion, try to find out why you did not succeed and profit by the lesson and resolve to do better next time.

RULE 5.—Accept responsibility whenever possible. Go out of your way to seek it. In this case, start with small responsibility and work your way up to greater responsibility.

RULE 6.—Whatever your present work may be, get a thorough grip of it in all its bearings. Get to know all you can about it; read, study, enquire of others; get all the information you can about your work and make up your mind to be an authority on it.

RULE 7.—If your mind is not in your work, *i.e.*, if you feel it is not the proper sphere for your talents, make a study of the work you would like to exchange into, and try all you can to grasp its requirements. Follow on the lines of Rule 5, and then, when opportunity comes to make an exchange, do not fear to grasp it even though it should at first mean a momentary sacrifice. If your judgment has been correct, and you have worked on the lines above, you will soon rise to higher things.

The second form of the fear of failure—that which attacks the man actually engaged in various spheres of work—is very important to the student of self-consciousness. It is a fear that operates in two ways, viz., suddenly or invidiously. We illustrated the sudden operation of this fear in dealing with stage-fright. We must now illustrate its insidious attack.

An author has worked for some time on a novel cr some other form of literary work, when one day in a pause there comes to him the thought: "I wonder if this book will take." He continues to work, and another day the thought comes again, and he listens to it with more attention. This time, perhaps, it unsettles him, or causes a break in his work. Day after day the thought returns, until gradually it changes its character. It now begins to assume the form: "I don't think this book will take; I feel it will not be a success." As time goes on the thought becomes so insistent that it begins to affect him. He gives more and more heed to the thought, until the future of his book is dark and dismal. Eventually, in despair, he puts it to one side as an utter failure.

If the insidious form of the fear of failure has ever brought disaster to you, we ask you to review the history of the thought, and you will note how it has gradually increased in power, until it has completed its destructive work.

There are four main causes for this insidious fear. It can be caused by (1) A difficulty, (2) fatigue, (3) ill-health, (4) low vitality. Let us look at these.

(1) If your work grows difficult or complicated, there is room for you to doubt your ability to cope with the difficulty or complication. When you begin to have doubts, an easy gradation leads to the thought of failure. (2) If you are fatigued, your enthusiasm for your work is apt to lessen, and anything that weakens your enthusiasm always encourages doubts or despair. (3) If your health is below par, you tend to paint things black, and this may extend to your work. (4) If your vitality is low, you are liable to attacks from all kinds of fear-thoughts, and you cannot think of things with the same brightness of outlook. A favorite time for low vitality to make its attack is in the middle hours of the night or very early morning. If you think of your work then you are very liable to see it in dismal coloring.

No matter from which of these causes your fear takes its start, you will find, on analysis, that it always proceeds by way of suggestion. Suggestion is at the root of the matter, and until it is attacked vigorously no cure is possible. I shall now give rules to overcome the force of this subtle suggestion, and so cure the insidious fear of failure.

RULE 1.—Whenever a failure-thought enters your mind refuse to dwell upon it; check it instantly; meet it by thoughts opposite in character.

RULE 2.—When you feel you have control over the failure-thought try to find out what has caused it. If you have good grounds for believing it to be due to fatigue, ill-health, or low vitality, you should recognize that the fear of failure is due solely to one of these causes and not **to any inherent** weakness or defect in your work. A full recognition of this by you will rob the failure-thought of any power over you. It is also advisable at such times, to leave your work (if possible) until you are thoroughly rested, or in a better state of health or vitality.

RULE 3.—If the failure-thought is due to a difficulty, or complexity in your work, do not get discouraged. Use auto-suggestion. Say to yourself: "I will leave this over for the present and return to it later, and then the difficulty will not trouble me, for I shall overcome it." I have found this to work wonders in my own case.

RULE 4.—When you find failure-thoughts continue to creep in when at your work, you will find it a good plan to use auto-suggestion before beginning work. Prepare yourself as follows: "I shall do well to-day with my work (specify what it is); everything will go smoothly. I am determined to make a success of this, and nothing shall turn me aside from it." It is always advisable to make the suggestion in your own language. The auto-suggestion must be YOU, YOU, YOU; it must be a part of yourself and thoroughly true to your nature if it is to be truly effective.

RULE 5.—Constantly spur yourself up with success-thoughts as you walk along the streets or in your walks in the country. Constant practice on these lines will make the success-thoughts part of your being.

RULE 6.—If you can see ahead that there is a difficulty waiting for you in your work, choose the time to deal with it when you feel in good trim; never attack difficulties when you are dispirited, tired, or low in vitality.

N. B.—Note the difference between fear of failure and knowledge of failure. The latter has no relation to fear; it is simply a recognition of the fact that something done *has* proved a failure or *will* prove a failure. The reason for the failure is perhaps known and will be guarded against in another attempt, or, where the reason is unknown, persistent endeavor will be made to discover it.

SECTION FORTY-TWO.

HOW TO CURE THE FEAR OF CRITICISM.

In *Section* 13 I divided critics into two classes—the narrow class—that of the real conscientious critic, the man really entitled to the name, and the wide class—the self-constituted critic, who criticizes everything and everybody. The narrow class may be termed true criticism, and the wide class I will term idle criticism. To clear the ground for the cure of criticism, let us try to determine its range.

Criticism may be directed against (1) Our person—appearances, dress, speech, or any bodily blemish or defect, (2) our actions—walk, mannerisms, gestures, etc., (3) our public life or our private life, (4) the exercise of our abilities or talents.

What attitude should I adopt towards criticism? I feel sure the following will appear to you to be reasonable. A criticism is either just or unjust. If it be just we shall be foolish to ignore it; if it be unjust we shall be foolish to pay heed to it. The man who is untroubled by self-consciousness may safely adopt this attitude towards criticism. If the criticism directed against him be just, he should obey it and fall in line with it. If it be unjust, he need not worry about it.

The self-conscious man is in a very different position. His mental attitude towards criticism is such that it affects his powers of reason and judgment. He cannot look at the matter fairly and squarely; he sums up (in general) criticism as an attempt to make him appear ridiculous. As a first step towards a change of mental attitude, I invite the self-conscious man who fears criticism to look at it in the following light. Try to realize, when you think people are criticizing you, that you are only a unit in a mass, one individual among a vast number of individuals. The mass cares very little about you—you are only a something on which the mass bestows a glance now and then. As a self-conscious being you are far too apt to emphasize the attention the mass pays to you. Try to grasp that the attention of the mass is only a momentary thing, and with this as a basis, I ask you to give careful consideration to the following rules:

RULE 1.—Try to realize that the great bulk of what you term criticism is simply idle criticism. It can hurt you only if you are foolish enough to allow it to hurt you. You must ignore it and turn your mind to thoughts more profitable to your well-being.

RULE 2.—Never allow your mind to dwell upon criticism directed against your person or your actions. Turn the table on your critics—CRITICIZE THEM. This will keep your mind from dwelling upon yourself and what others may be thinking of you.

RULE 3.—When criticism is directed against your talents or abilities be concerned about one thing only, viz., whether the criticism is just or unjust. If it be just, seek to profit by it; if it be unjust, dismiss it from your thoughts. Note—Do not attempt to deal with a criticism when under the sway of emotion; leave it until you can deal with it in a calm, collected frame of mind.

RULE 4.—Do not be afraid of the criticism of an audience; on the whole, it is kind. The audience would much rather see you do well than badly. They have come to get value for their money, and if you can give them even a little satisfaction they will soon show you their appreciation. Go before them prepared to do your best, and even should you do badly, or fail completely, it is not a deadly matter, for your audience will soon forget all about you. If you doubt this, ask an advertiser; he will tell you all about the short memory of the public.

RULE 5.—Do all you can to improve your powers of self-reliance and self-confidence. Strengthen your power of inhibition by constant practice. Pay special heed to the control of your emotions, and above all, neglect no opportunity of practicing thought-control, and the fear of criticism will cease to trouble you.

Read in connection with this section—"How To Cure The Fear Of Ridicule."

SECTION FORTY-THREE.

HOW TO CURE THE FEAR OF COMPANY (SOCIAL LIFE).

To cure the fear of company is generally looked upon by self-conscious people as almost an impossibility. The reason of this lies in this fear being of the class of fears where we fear people in the mass. The self-conscious man feels in presence of this fear that he is in very truth a "fearer," (*Section* 3) a traveler away from home. It, therefore, raises all his primitive distrust of people who are strangers to him or with whom he is not well acquainted.

Taking this fear of people in the mass as the basic cause of the fear of company, we have besides four common causes of this fear. Thus, the fear of company may be due to (*a*) Timidity and shyness, (*b*) the nature of the company, *i.e.*, society to which you are strange or unaccustomed, (*c*) lowness of tone, physically and mentally, passing into actual nervousness, (*d*) uncertainty as to your welcome, both prior to meeting the company or when actually among them.

In dealing with the cure of the fear of company, we have to keep in mind its two-fold aspect—(1) Fear prior to going into company, and (2) fear when actually in company.

You saw (*Section* 14) that (1) was always attended by prefunctioning, which though necessarily dim and vague, nevertheless caused a certain degree of nervous strain, and a feeling of great unrest during the whole of the period prior to the engagement; (2) was found to be largely determined by the people you meet, and the chance of situations arising for which you are totally unprepared, thus leading to the fear of the unexpected.

If you will take into account the causes of the fear of company and its two-fold aspect, you will see that the fear of company is a complex fear involving many factors. In view of this I strongly advise all who wish to overcome the fear of company to give themselves a good grounding in the instruction laid down in Chapter I, PART TWO —"PRELIMINARY TRAINING FOR THE CURE OF SELF-CONSCIOUSNESS." Very special attention should be paid to *Sections* 31, 32, 33, and 35. The discipline given in this training will be invaluable, for it gives a solid basis on which to build a real and lasting cure. After the training above has been carried out with a fair degree of success, the following rules will be found useful:

RULE 1.—If you find that a great deal of your fear of company is due to prefunctioning you should use prefunctioning to cure your fear. Follow on the lines given in *Section* 39. Imagine that you see yourself meeting the company. Imagine that you see yourself calm, cool and collected, and everything passing off well. To enable you to visualize this, bring back to your memory company in which you have figured lately. Review the scene with your mind's eye until you see yourself acting as you could have wished you had acted. Never picture your failures; blot them out and picture instead a success.

RULE 2.—Apart from prefunctioning, cultivate a strong belief in your ability to go into company with a firm faith in your power to hold your own. Never allow any doubt of this to trouble you, *i.e.*, as soon as such a doubt enters your mind refuse to dwell upon it; switch the mind at once to other thoughts. Cultivate, also, the belief that the actual company will not be so dreadful as the ideal company—the company pictured by your imagination.

RULE 3.—Remember what I said in *Section* 39, under

Rule 4, about the imitative faculty of an audience. If you go into company nervous, ill at ease, timid, and shy, you make the company feel similarly towards you. If you approach the company in a spirit of good humor, endeavoring to make yourself agreeable to all with whom you come into contact, and back this up with courtesy and politeness you will find the company meet you halfway. You will find, also, that the good humor which you have assumed will rapidly give way to genuine good humor and then your success with the company is assured unless it be extra stiff and formal. You will find, also, that if you should happen to make a few blunders, much will be forgiven you on account of your attitude towards the company.

RULE 4.—Guard against paying too much attention to your movements, such as walking across a room or passing anything at table. Attention to movements that are habitual to you robs them of their automaticity and makes them appear awkward.

Read also in connection with this section, "How To Control The Fear Of The Unexpected."

SECTION FORTY-FOUR.

HOW TO CURE THE FEAR OF INTERVIEWS.

This fear is so common, so well known, that it is unnecessary to go beyond the details given in *Section* 15. Like so many of the fears we have dealt with, it is dual in character. Thus we have fear prior to the interview, and fear during the interview. Where the person you are going to see is unknown to you, your fear is mainly due to prefunctioning, imagining all kinds of dreadful things concerning him. Where the person is known to you, your fear is purely self-conscious fear, or fear as regards the outcome of the interview.

If the fear of interviews troubles you, I cannot give you better advice than to get a good grounding in the discipline given in "PRELIMINARY TRAINING FOR THE CURE OF SELF-CONSCIOUSNESS," PART TWO, Chapter I., and then you must proceed on the lines of the following rules:

RULE 1.—If prefunctioning is at the root of your fear, stop imagining all kinds of dreadful possibilities at the interview. Use prefunctioning by picturing everything passing off well, and back up the prefunctioning by auto-suggestion. Say to yourself: "I shall come out of this interview all right. Everything will be satisfactory." Do not use these actual words; make suggestions to fit the case so as to give them more force, and remember to say them with deep conviction and earnestness.

RULE 2.—Go to the interview with a strong feeling of confidence in yourself. If you have carried out the instructions in *Section* 35 this should not be difficult. Stop at once any tendency to dwell on thoughts of nervousness or timidity. Use auto-suggestion to the effect that you have thorough command over yourself.

RULE 3.—If you know the person you are going to see, do not dwell on anything connected with him likely to cause you to fear him. Inhibit such thoughts at once. Dwell on your belief in yourself; think of yourself as one going to victory, one who is sure to conquer.

RULE 4.—When you are speaking at the interview, look your man squarely in the face and speak with deliberation, with the feeling behind the words that you are making an impression, making your personality tell. Let your manner be pleasant, polite, and strictly in keeping with the occasion.

RULE 5.—Make a practice of rehearsing what you will say at the interview, in the privacy of your own room, in as few words as possible. The rehearsal is very important for it accustoms you to the sound of your own voice, thus removing one of the sources of fear-thoughts.

RULE 6.—As far as possible, go to the interview thoroughly prepared. Have everything relative to it at your finger ends.

SECTION FORTY-FIVE.

HOW TO CURE FEAR IN BUSINESS.

In laying down rules for the cure of fear in business, I shall take as my basis the beginnings of this fear. That is to say, all rules will be made specially applicable to young people just beginning a business career. With regard to people who have been in business for some time, and are still troubled with the fear of business, it will be easy for them to adapt the rules to their own special needs.

In *Section* 16 I took five typical modes of the fear of business, and we feel sure that it will be more useful and more satisfactory to give separate rules for each mode rather than general rules for the various modes. I shall take them in the order given in *Section* 16.

(*a*) RULES FOR CURING THE FEAR OF EMPLOYERS, SUPERIORS, ETC.

RULE 1.—As the root of this fear is the idea that your employer or superior is constantly watching you, you must inhibit this idea. Concentrate your mind upon your work and the best way to do it. The better you are able to concentrate, the less will the watchful eye of your employer trouble you.

RULE 2.—Go to business each day with the strong determination to do your work well. As far as possible, have your work for the day mapped out beforehand, so that you can start upon it right away.

RULE 3.—Cultivate a strong belief in your ability to do your work well under all conditions. Remember that lack of confidence weakens your working power, and provides an avenue for fear-thoughts.

(b) RULES FOR CURING THE FEAR OF CUSTOMERS.

RULE 1.—Make a study of each type of customer so that you may know the right approach, and the right way to handle him. Do not make the fatal mistake of a hard and fast mode of address for each customer. If you regard each customer as a separate study your fear of the customer will sink into the background. It will pay you to study books on Salesmanship, and also business magazines like *"System."*

RULE 2.—Never dwell on doubts of your ability to handle a customer. Feel that there is a way to deal with him, and that it is your business to discover that way. Do not allow occasional failures with customers to depress you. Regard each failure as a stimulus to further effort. Study your failures, and try to discover why you failed and how you should have proceeded.

RULE 3.—Never lose your temper with a customer. The desire to "have a shot at him" if carried into effect is time wasted. Look at him as simply a "subject" to be handled successfully. Look at each customer from a development point of view—this lessens the risk of losing your temper. You must aim at coming out of each difficult situation stronger than when you entered.

RULE 4.—Never allow yourself to get flurried with a customer. Cultivate quick, quiet, methodical ways of working. Use auto-suggestion if you find any tendency to flurry. Say to yourself: "I am cool, calm, and collected. I have perfect control over myself. I shall deal with this customer successfully."

(c) RULES FOR CURING THE FEAR OF RESPONSIBILITY.

RULE 1.—Prepare for responsibility by seeing it coming. There is a way to do this. From the first day of your entry into business make it a point to learn all you can about that business. Take for your motto, "Knowledge drives out Fear.'' When you know how to do a thing you will not be afraid to do it, therefore, get all the knowledge you can of your business. Cherish the opportunities you get to do something new. You will not be asked to do big things right away, so attack the little things with confidence, and when the big things come they will not appear big, for you will have approached them by graduated steps.

RULE 2.—Seek opportunities to mix with your fellow employees who are doing work different from your own in the firm. Be tactful and employ skillful questioning so that you may grasp the nature of their work and the best methods of doing it. Guard against any appearance of being inquisitive; let all your search for information be perfectly honest and natural, and be ready to give information yourself, whenever it is right and proper to do so.

RULE 3.—When you have to do any work strange to you approach it in a spirit of confidence for this will preserve your energies. Use auto-suggestion to the effect that you will manage the new work all right.

RULE 4.—When advice is given to you by superiors pay attention to it and seek to see what lies behind the advice. Make constant use of your thinking powers so that you may work not blindly but with judgment.

(d) RULES FOR CURING THE FEAR OF RUSH-PERIODS.

RULE 1.—Prepare for rush-periods by trying to do your work well and quickly at ordinary times. See to it that everything is planned out, as far as possible, and arranged methodically.

RULE 2.—In speeding up your work be careful to guard against strain and the FEELING of strain. Let your mental attitude be one of calmness. The more calmly you are able to work, the easier will you find it to increase your speed.

RULE 3.—Look forward to rush-periods with a spirit of confidence. After your first experience of a rush-period make what measure of success you have had the basis for your next rush-period. Cheer yourself up with auto-suggestion: ''I did well last time and I will do well again this time.'' Many have found this attitude towards the rush-period work like a charm.

(e) RULES FOR CURING THE FEAR OF LOSING YOUR EMPLOYMENT.

RULE 1.—Make yourself valuable to your firm by always doing your work well, and by using initiative. Try to see ahead so that you may plan to keep the business-ball rolling.

RULE 2.—Try to save something out of your income so that if the worst should come you would not starve. But remember this—you must on no account think of or look forward to the worst coming. Always keep hold of the thought that the best is coming. Inhibit every thought of loss of employment, for such thoughts weaken your working power.

RULE 3.—Try to have more than one string to your bow. In your leisure hours improve your mind and have some useful hobby that will bring you in spare cash. Encourage and cultivate the feeling that no matter what happens you will come out all right. Remember that I do not mean that you are to indulge in day-dreaming. I want you to back up the spirit of confidence in the future by hard thinking, planning, and WORK.

I hope you will understand that my object in all the above rules is to make you lose yourself in your business. When you grasp that the acquirement of a sound knowledge of your business, and the best ways of doing your work are the surest means of curing your business fears, you will do your utmost to work on the lines I have laid down.

SECTION FORTY-SIX.

HOW TO CONTROL THE FEAR OF THE UNEXPECTED.

In our analysis of the fear of the unexpected (*Section* 17) we saw that there were two forms of it. (*a*) The fear that comes through the knowledge that the unexpected *does* happen to us, and (*b*) the fear that arises through the actual happening or presence of the unexpected. The first form we saw was either an ever-present fear, or a fear recurrent at special times or on special occasions. The second form we found to be the *real* fear of the unexpected. The first of these two forms is curable in its early stages. As regards the second form, all that you should strive for is to control it. I shall examine each form, therefore, in the light of what I said in my analysis, and give separate rules for each—rules for the cure of the early stages of form (*a*), and rules for the control of form (*b*).

(*a*) This form of the fear of the unexpected may be traced either to your having been present at some happening where the unexpected has occurred, or it may arise from reading or hearing of some event where the unexpected happened. In either case the fear reveals itself as a dread of danger coming in an unexpected form. At this stage the fear attacks one only at special times or on special occasions, but if this attitude towards danger is encouraged, *i.e.*, dwelt upon, it tends to become an obsession, and either you are in constant dread of danger coming in some unexpected way, or you are constantly attempting to foreshadow or foresee how the danger will come to you. You are then in the absurd position of expecting the unexpected. The obsession stage is difficult to cure, and I shall not attempt it here. Cases of this nature should be entrusted to a qualified mind-specialist with a sound knowledge of psychotherapy. It will be understood that the rules below apply simply to the early stages of form (*a*).

RULES FOR THE CURE OF THE FEAR THAT COMES TO US THROUGH THE KNOWLEDGE THAT THE UNEXPECTED DOES HAPPEN TO US.

RULE 1.—Lie down on a couch or sofa, in the privacy of your own room. Concentrate for a few minutes on the thought that you are resting. Repeat to yourself, "I am resting, resting." Next, turn your mind to the event, happening, or other cause responsible for your fear of the unexpected. Review the matter minutely and reason with yourself on the folly of letting such ideas have an influence over you. Repeat this process each day at the same hour (as far as possible) for a week. When you get up from the couch dismiss from your mind all thought of what you have been doing and seek company or read an interesting book so as to divert your mind from the thought of the fear.

RULE 2.—If the fear-thought still comes into your mind during the day after practicing the exercise above, you must try to pass the thought on. Think of something else at once; get to work on something that will engage your mind as fully as possible.

RULE 3.—If the fear-thought continues to worry you I ask you to think of the fear from an insurance point of view. Suppose, for instance, your fear takes the form of a constant dread of fire whenever you go to a picture-hall or theater. If you were to ask "Lloyds" to insure you against such a fate your premium would be very light. For consider: think of the thousands upon thousands of performances that take place every night, and then think of the very few cases of fire that occur even in a whole year. The chances are several millions to one against such a fate as you imagine ever being yours.

RULE 4.—Cultivate a fearless attitude towards life. Consider how short life is even at its longest. Resolve that you will fear nothing, that you will enjoy life to the full. Make constant use of auto-suggestion to strengthen your resolve.

RULE 5.—Guard against fatigue, for it is a favorite condition of body and mind for fear-thoughts to operate on. Do all you can to strengthen your body. Take plenty of exercise, eat nourishing food, and get all the fresh air you can.

(*b*) This form of the fear of the unexpected is always dramatic in its suddenness. It comes like a flash, and therefore demands lightning methods of control. In *Section* 17 I gave five specific ways in which the fear of the unexpected can make its attack. The list is by no means exhaustive, and is meant merely to illustrate some of the ways in which the fear may come to us.

If you will examine these typical instances carefully, you will note that in each case there is great mental agitation at the moment when the fear makes its attack. The bodily disturbance follows by reflex action, but no matter how severe this may be, the mind has always the greater share of the pain to bear. It will be evident to you, therefore, that it is the control of the mind that is the important factor in dealing with the real fear of the unexpected. If we can control the mind, the body will be able to take care of itself. I ask your attention, therefore, to the following rules:

RULES FOR CONTROLLING THE FEAR THAT ARISES FROM THE ACTUAL HAPPENING OR PRESENCE OF THE UNEXPECTED.

RULE 1.—Your attitude towards the fear of the unexpected must be one of preparedness. In other words, you must have at hand the cool, calm, collected frame of mind. This mental attitude must be cultivated diligently until it becomes habitual to you. To secure this end you must have a thorough grip of the training given in the following sections of this book, viz., *Sections* 30, 31, 32, 33, 35, 37. To enforce the ideas given in these sections, *Section* 34 must have very careful study.

RULE 2.—When the fear of the unexpected makes its attack you will find it very helpful to recognize it as such. That is to say, you must KNOW that you have been attacked by the unexpected and tell yourself this. Say to yourself: "This is the fear of the unexpected; I must be cool, calm, and collected, resolute and brave." If you have cultivated the attitude of mind embodied in this affirmation, it will come to your aid the instant you recognize the nature of the fear. I attach great importance to this recognition of the fear for I have proved its value on several occasions. The recognition is a check to the mental disturbance which you must follow up by inhibiting the thought of fear. You must then give your attention to the control of your muscles, especially of the facial muscles.

RULE 3.—If the fear of the unexpected comes through your having made a mistake, blunder, or miscalculation, as soon as you have carried out the instructions in the preceding rule you must at once try to repair or remedy the mistake, etc. If it be irreparable, you must plan at once to lessen the consequences of your fault, as far as possible. The great thing to strive for is to get your critical faculties—your powers of thinking, weighing up, judging, to work at once. The better you are able to do this, the better will you be able to overcome the emotional disturbance; for you should recognize that your critical faculties and your emotional powers do not work well together; one of them MUST have the upper hand.

RULE 4.—Where the emotional stress is very severe so that the critical faculties are pushed into the background, and where there is no immediate action necessary (such as having to repair a mistake) it is best to try to turn the mind into other channels so as to give the emotions time to subside. From what I have said already in the course of this book you will know what means will be best for this turning of the mind aside from your fear.

It is impossible to give rules to meet every case of the fear of the unexpected, but I feel sure that the diligent student of this book will make a splendid fight when his turn comes to face the fear of the unexpected.

CHAPTER VII.

TIMIDITY AND BASHFULNESS.

SECTION FORTY-SEVEN.
THE CURE OF THE SECONDARY CAUSES OF SELF-CONSCIOUSNESS.

The secondary causes of self-consciousness are of fundamental importance, for they are bound up with so many forms of fear that it is absolutely necessary for self-conscious persons to stamp them out if they are to make real progress towards getting rid of their self-consciousness. I cannot advise you too strongly, therefore, to examine yourself thoroughly, and where you are conscious that any of these secondary causes apply to your case, you should do your utmost to overcome them by carrying out my instructions on the lines I have laid down. The rules and exercises for the cure of the various secondary causes are thoroughly practical, and are founded on experience and a careful study of the subject, and I can guarantee their effectiveness to achieve their objective.

Success is certain to everyone who will be guided by my advice, and whenever a student feels any inclination to despair or doubt, I ask him to look at such despair or doubt as purely temporary, and certain to disappear if he will persevere with the rules and exercises provided for him. He should encourage himself constantly with the idea that success is certain if he continues his efforts. Further, he should make constant use of auto-suggestion to enforce the idea of success. Where success is looked forward to, expected, and *worked* for, on proper lines, success is bound to come.

SECTION FORTY-EIGHT.

HOW TO CURE TIMIDITY.

In reading the lives of great men, one is often struck by the fact that some of the world's bravest men were in their early days very timid individuals. This should be remembered by timid people. It should prove a stimulus to them to make an effort to cast off their timidity.

I described (*Section* 19) timidity as a habit of mind, something that has grown from small beginnings. It is true that some people seem predisposed, through hereditary influences, to timidity; but even in their case their timidity is a process of slow growth. Very timid people often put this forward as an excuse for their timidity. They will tell you (or more often they say it to themselves) that they were "born timid," all their people are timid, and therefore they cannot help being timid. These people forget, however, that even if they were "born timid," or with a disposition towards timidity, this is not their sole heritage. Every man is born with numerous instincts, among which are the fighting instincts, such as pugnacity and assertiveness. Yes, even timid people are born with these instincts, and when these instincts are aroused timidity has to take a back seat. The timid man becomes bold and brave, and on occasion can be a warrior bold when under the influence of the fighting instincts.

Here is a curious fact, *and it is a very encouraging fact to the timid man.* No matter how timid or unaggressive a man's habitual nature may be, under hypnosis he acts as a confident, resolute man will behave.

What messages does this suggestive fact bring to you? I feel sure that if you will reflect upon it, it will bring to you this message: "If I like, I can, by calling into being the deeper forces of my nature, get rid of my timidity, whether hereditary or otherwise." That is the message this suggestive fact brings to you, and it should encourage you to make this call on the deeper forces of your nature.

To aid you in this worthy work, I ask you to give faithful practice to the following rules, and I guarantee you will get rid of your timidity, *and stand forth a courageous and resolute individual.*

RULE 1.—As a first step towards your cure, get rid once and for all of the idea that people are always trying to make you look small or to make a fool of you. Inhibit these ideas the instant they enter the mind.

RULE 2.—Cultivate from now a spirit of boldness and fearlessness. Here is a useful little exercise that will help you to do this. EXERCISE: Stand in front of a wardrobe mirror. Draw yourself up erect with your hands down by your sides, and then use auto-suggestion. Say to yourself: "I feel much braver to-day. I feel more resolute, more courageous. I have more confidence in myself." Make phrases like these and repeat them with great earnestness. After a few minutes drop the exercise, and then try to carry a little of the spirit of your auto-suggestion out with you into the great world of your everyday activities.

RULE 3.—Practice for a short time each day some form of physical exercise so that you may improve your physique, and tone up your system.

RULE 4.—Practice looking at people you meet in the street, or in business, with a fearless glance. Let the glance be swift at first, and as you gain confidence gradually extend the length until you can look at a person and engage in talk with him without any feeling of timidity. In looking at people, look at them straight between the eyes; let your manner be pleasant and courteous. Encourage the feeling that you are not afraid to look at anyone.

RULE 5.—Practice reading aloud and thinking aloud when alone so as to get accustomed to the sound of your own voice. Imagine you are talking to people, telling a story, or describing something you have seen or heard about. Getting accustomed to the sound of your own voice will take away a great deal of your fear when talking to people.

RULE 6.—This rule is the most important of all. Fight your timidity by going where you now shrink from going. Thus, when you go to a meeting do not slink into the back seats; go boldly up to the front seats. Similarly, in company, do not hang about the door of the room, sliding into the first chair and sitting on the edge as if afraid to trust your weight to the chair. Get well into the room and mix with the company boldly. At first you will probably find this course of action difficult, but I can assure you it will not be VERY difficult if you have practiced the preceding rules in this section. You will find, also, that with every attempt it will be easier for you to act as I have directed; then the time will come when you will feel a pleasant thrill go through you as you make your way to the front conscious that you have got rid of your timidity. This rule, at a first glance, may seem to many people (especially young ladies) horrid, brutal, and awful, but it MUST be done if you are to conquer your timidity. Remember, it is only the first plunge or two that is difficult, and it is surely worth the effort to get rid of your self-distrust. Better a few minutes of agony (if you like to term it so) than a lifetime of misery due to your timid fears.

SECTION FORTY-NINE.

HOW TO CURE SHYNESS.

It is related of one of a great statesman that he was so shy that often rather than meet anyone but those with whom he was on intimate terms, he would stop and look in a shop window, and pretend to be greatly interested in its contents, or if time permitted, he would turn aside and walk off in another direction.

Instances like this are more common than one would suppose. Many men of the greatest ability are so cursed with shyness that they will do anything rather than mix with people who are not intimate acquaintances. A strange thing about many people of this class is that at times they seem to come out of their shell of shyness, and then they strike you as bold, fearless men. At such times, a stranger seeing them would never dream of thinking of them as shy; their bearing is entirely opposed to such a conception of them.

From a careful study and observation of shy people, I make bold to say that shy people are really people who are at heart brave and courageous; they only require the right stimulus to show themselves to the world in their true colors. I ask every shy person, therefore, to believe that it *is* possible for him to get rid of his shyness. All that is required is that he will endeavor to make every effort to overcome his trouble. *Success is certain if he will persevere on the lines of the following rules:*

RULE 1.—As a preliminary, get a good grip of *Sections* 31, 32, 35, and 37. Enforce these ideas by a thorough knowledge of *Section* 34.

RULE 2.—As the chief characteristic of shyness is a shrinking feeling, a shrinking up into yourself, you must check this feeling whenever you experience it. Instead of shrinking, or stepping back from meeting a person, GO FORWARD. Force yourself to do this; go forward with confidence and meet the person. If you have carried out my instructions in the *Sections* under RULE 1, it will not be so difficult for you to meet people as you are now apt to imagine. I can assure you, too, that with every effort you will find it easier to carry out.

RULE 3.—If the shrinking feeling is experienced only when you meet certain people or a certain class of people, you should use prefunctioning to help you. In the privacy of your own room, lie down with eyes closed and imagine yourself meeting these people who cause you to be shy. See yourself going up to them, or bowing to them in passing, without any sensation of the shrinking feeling. Visualize the scene as vividly as possible until the people stand out with the clearness of real life and then use auto-suggestion, such as: "Next time I meet you, Mr. X., I shall be perfectly easy and natural in your presence. I shall be quite at my ease." If you feel shy in the presence of servants or subordinates, especially when giving them orders, use prefunctioning and auto-suggestion exactly on the same lines.

RULE 4.—If your shyness is caused by any facial blemish, or any physical defect, inhibit such thoughts as soon as they enter your mind. People will overlook these if you try to make your personality strong, cheery, and genial. If you doubt this, look around you and observe how people who have these defects are still pronounced a social success. Watch these people, study them, and you will get many a helpful hint.

RULE 5.—If your shyness is due to some secret sin (real or imaginary) or to some defect of speech, do all you can to remove each cause. Be determined not to let it prove a stumbling-block to you.

You are advised to practice in conjunction with the above, RULES 4, 5, and 6 in "How To Cure Timidity."

SECTION FIFTY.

HOW TO CURE BASHFULNESS.

The prominent feature of bashfulness is the downcast look. It works in a manner almost similar to reflex action. As soon as a bashful person meets the gaze of another person, or thinks that another person is looking at him, instantly his eyes take the downcast look.

I have said in *Section* 21 that bashfulness is a state of feeling. The bashful person feels that he is bashful, and this feeling affects his whole mentality. He cannot think when under the spell of bashfulness; he gets confused, his speech is hesitating, his whole mind and body are affected.

I ask every bashful person to believe that he *can* cure his bashfulness if he will only make up his mind to try. If he will give diligent practice to the rules and exercises below, I guarantee him success. I ask him to encourage himself with the thought that the effort is well worth his while. With his bashfulness out of the way, he will be able to take his proper place in society, and he will have removed one of the greatest hindrances to his success in business or in professional life.

Rule 1.—From the present moment, never admit to yourself or to any other person that you are bashful. Inhibit such thoughts at once.

Rule 2.—Do all you can to improve your self-reliance and self-confidence (see *Section* 35 (*a*) (*b*)). Cultivate a spirit of fearlessness and use auto-suggestion to help you. (See Rule 2, *Section* 48.)

Rule 3.—Resist every tendency to lower your gaze when you meet people, or to shrink from meeting them. The following exercises are intended as a preliminary training to this end, and after practicing them for a week or two, you should commence looking with a fearless gaze at the people you meet in everyday life.

Exercise (a). Procure a number of photographs or reproductions of photographs in magazines and sit down at your ease and proceed to examine each photograph with great care. Center your gaze upon the eyes of the person or persons in the photograph. Try to imagine that they are real, living people, who are looking at YOU, and that you are gazing back at them intently and without any tendency to shrink from their gaze. Use auto-suggestion while you are looking at the photograph. Repeat to yourself: ''I can look at you (*i.e.*, the person in the photograph) quite calmly. I can meet your gaze fearlessly.'' If, while you say these words, you feel the uneasy sensation which usually follows when you look at a real person, check this feeling instantly. Simulate instead, a feeling of pleasure and joy. Practice this exercise a few minutes each day.

Exercise (b). Sit in front of a mirror and gaze steadily into your right eye, then shift your gaze to the left eye; next gaze at an imaginary point between the two eyes. While you are looking into the mirror try to imagine that you are looking at a stranger, and that you are able to look at him without blinking, and quite fearlessly. Some people find it a good plan to alter the expression of their face so as to appear fierce, proud, angry, disdainful, etc., while looking in the glass, at the same time simulating the feeling that they are looking at a stranger (under these conditions) who is unable to affect them.

RULE 4.—In practicing exercise (a) as above, I told you to imagine that the photographs were real people. I wish you to reverse this now. When you look at real people imagine THEY are photographs. This attitude towards them, although it may strike you as strange, tends to give you the same mental quiet which you experienced when looking at the photographs.

As bashfulness is often associated with timidity and shyness, you should read these sections carefully, and where the rules of cure apply to your case you should put them into practice along with the rules in this section.

SECTION FIFTY-ONE.

HOW TO CURE STAMMERING AND STUTTERING.

Stammering and stuttering are so closely akin that so far as this book is concerned it is unnecessary to differentiate in laying down rules for their cure. For it will be remembered that in *Section* 22 I said that by far the greater number of cases of stammering and stuttering are due to mental causes.   And as these mental causes are all related to some form of fear, particularly that class of fears to which self-conscious people are specially liable, they are more amenable to successful treatment than cases due to physical causes.

Personally, I incline to the belief that stuttering is purely mental in origin, and hence is curable if the stutterer will submit to the necessary discipline.   With regard to stammering, the case is different; in some cases (the majority) it is due to mental causes, and in other cases to physical causes.   Where stammering is due to the latter it is difficult to hold out hopes of a cure.   Where the physical cause is fever, ill-health, epilepsy, hysteria, there may be *some* hope of a cure, but where the physical cause is some obscure congenital defect, some malformation of the mouth, tongue, or tonsils, the most that can be hoped for is some improvement.   Various methods have been tried to overcome this malformation, such as by surgical operations, altering the setting of the teeth, and experiments with the tongue in various positions in the mouth.   As stated before (*Section* 22), whenever the cause is physical, its treatment should be in the hands of one who has specialized on the subject.

I shall now proceed to give rules for the cure of stammering and stuttering when due to mental causes, and I earnestly hope that persons who are troubled in this way will give the rules careful and diligent practice.   Just one word before I pass to the rules.   If you are in doubt as to the cause of your stammering, you should visit your doctor, and let him examine your mouth, tongue, tonsils, teeth, throat.   If there is a malformation of these he will be able to tell you.

RULE 1.—It is essential, at the outset, to cultivate the belief that you can speak EVERY word, and speak it under all kinds of conditions.   Use auto-suggestion such as: "I know that I can speak every word under all conditions, if

I set my mind to it. I am determined to do this.'' Repeat this with great earnestness every day, at frequent intervals.

RULE 2.—Read aloud for ten minutes every day. Read slowly and deliberately, carefully pronouncing each syllable.

RULE 3.—In reading aloud, take note of those letters or combination of letters that cause you trouble. Make a list of them and repeat them over and over several times each day. In the course of time, when you come across these letters in reading or in speaking you will say them naturally without any stumbling. Your motor memory will have become automatic and you will utter these letters without conscious attention.

RULE 4.—When speaking to anyone DO NOT THINK OF YOUR UTTERANCE; keep your mind on the matter. You will speak fluently if you keep your mind on what you are saying, not on how you are saying it.

RULE 5.—Cultivate a pleasant manner in speaking. If you do this people will not think so much of your slips or defects of utterance, and you will not have the same mental confusion.

RULE 6.—Guard against excitement or giving way to emotion in speaking, for this tends to affect your utterance. Make it a rule to keep your speaking-voice within the middle register of your voice. This will give you greater control over your voice.

RULE 7.—Never think of your trouble (stammering or stuttering) when speaking to anyone. Inhibit such thoughts or words instantly.

RULE 8.—Never dwell on your lapses for this will most surely work upon you emotionally. Just say to yourself pleasantly, after each lapse: ''I shall do better next time,'' and then dismiss the thought of your lapse from your mind.

RULE 9.—Get a few lessons in singing from a good teacher of the art. This will be of great advantage to you, for you will get a good training in voice production, and in the art of breathing. Correct respiration has an important bearing on your trouble.

RULE 10.—Practice all kinds of vocal catches such as *"The great gray brigade," "She sells sea shells," "Truly rural," "Six sieves of sifted thistles," "Seven Severn salmon," "Betty Botha bought some butter," "The slack black stacks the stalks," "Black block click clock," "Lily blue flew true."* Repeat each phrase six times, as fast as possible. *N. B.—Do not practice any of the above until you have had a fair amount of practice at reading aloud.*

RULE 11.—Do all you can to improve your general health. When your vitality is low you are more liable to lapses than when your health is good.

RULE 12.—Try to get the co-operation of a friend, in sympathy with your efforts to overcome your trouble. After a good deal of private practice, read aloud to your friend; this will tend to give you more confidence in yourself when speaking to strangers.

SECTION FIFTY-TWO.

HOW TO CURE BLUSHING.

From the attitude I took up in *Section* 23, it will be understood that when I speak of curing blushing I am referring almost entirely to that common form of it which we named the self-conscious blush.   The other types I mentioned—the blush of shame or humiliation, the blush of anger, and the blush of love, do not come within our province.   There is, however, another form of blushing which I hinted at in *Section* 23, which I may term the semi-self-conscious blush.   It was this form I had in mind when I said that I doubted the existence of any man or woman who had never blushed, or that nothing on earth could make blush, and also when I spoke of the bearing of ill-health on blushing.   The stimulus can come in such subtle forms that sometimes the blush is there before we are aware of it. This semi-self-conscious blush is due partly to self-consciousness, and also to some hidden factor working through the feelings. Owing to its sudden and unexpected character, it cannot be cured, but it *can* be controlled, and I shall have to deal with it in separate rules.

(*a*) Rules For The Cure Of The Self-Conscious Blush.

Rule 1.—The first essential is to get a good grip of the training given in *Sections* 30 to 35. Special attention must be given to *Section* 35, for it is of the utmost importance.

Rule 2.—From the present moment resolve that you will not dwell upon the thought of blushing or the thought of the pain and annoyance it has caused you in the past. Whenever you find your mind tending to such thoughts inhibit them instantly and turn your mind into some other channel.

Rule 3.—Practice Rules 3 and 4 in *Section* 50 until you have a good grip of them.

Rule 4.—If you feel a tendency to blush when approaching anyone, either out of doors or in company, try by sheer force of will to control the feeling. This can be cultivated, and success will come in varying degree with repeated effort. You will find it helpful, after making the effort of will, to turn your thoughts to what you will say to the person who is approaching you. Check any tendency to think of yourself.

Rule 5.—Practice meeting people with a frank, pleasant, agreeable manner, for to do this PROPERLY you must of necessity turn your mind away from yourself. Your manner will not appeal to others unless you are thinking of THEM. This gives life and reality to your manner.

Rule 6.—When talking to strangers or to anyone who tends to make you blush, NEVER think of yourself. While you are speaking think solely of what you are saying. Never give a thought to what the stranger may be thinking of you. While HE is speaking adopt a keen listening attitude. (This can be cultivated to a great extent.) While YOU are listening, if you note any tendency on your part to think of yourself, or what the speaker may be thinking of you, check this instantly. Confine your thoughts to the conversation. Note the tones of the speaker's voice; note any peculiarity of pronunciation, note the construction of his sentences. Do anything, in fact, that will take your mind off yourself. Be determined that you will NOT think of yourself.

RULE 7.—Read carefully *Section* 43, and put into practice all the rules which you feel apply to you individually.

RULE 8.—As the self-conscious blush is intimately connected with many of the other secondary causes of self-consciousness, you must try to discover what part they play in making you blush. Make up your mind that you will root out timidity, shyness, and bashfulness from your personality, and resolve that the fear of ridicule and the fear of the ludicrous shall have no power over you.

Young men and young women are advised to read Section 56 in conjunction with the above rules.

(b) RULES FOR THE CONTROL OF THE SEMI-SELF-CONSCIOUS BLUSH.

RULE 1.—If you feel you are about to blush (and sometimes it is possible to have this feeling for quite an appreciable time in advance) try to check it by sheer force of will. Some people are able to do this very well indeed, only a very slight flush being traceable to a keen observer. Others have lesser degrees of success down to the man who is utterly unable to restrain the blush. I advise everyone, no matter what their degree of success or failure may be on any occasion, to continue, as occasion occurs, to try to check the blush by sheer force of will. The effort tends to rouse one's fighting instincts. It is a check to timidity and shyness. It tends also to rouse our inventive powers— we seek to invent new ideas and situations to occupy the mind, so as to escape the mental confusion which follows on the heels of the blush.

Rule 2.—If the blush springs into being before you have a chance to check it, you must aim now at controlling the mental confusion. Everyone has seen how this works. The brain is overwhelmed, we become dazed and lose our presence of mind, we cannot command our thoughts or give utterance to a word, and we feel intense mortification at our ridiculous position. To control the mental confusion you must simulate instantly a pleasant manner (allowance must be made for the particular occasion) and try to divert the mind into any channel but that connected with your blushing. You must inhibit this at once by concentrating your mind on some other thought. As the blushing always occurs when you are in the presence of other people, concentrate upon what they are saying or how they are saying it. Or you can concentrate your mind on their dress—the material, quality, style, finish. Pass on from thoughts like these to any object near at hand and concentrate upon that. You will understand that all this diversion of the mind from the thought of your blushing is necessary only for a short time. If you can keep your mind from thinking of your blushing for a minute or two, the flush will soon subside and you will at once feel easier. Be determined at the critical moment not to allow the mental confusion to run its course. Steady your mind by concentrating as above, and you will find that you will never lose your grip of yourself.

Rule 3.—It is a good plan, after one of these sudden blushing attacks, to review an hour or two afterwards the whole of the experience, *i.e.*, the surroundings and situation that led to the attack, and the character of the mental process and mental disturbance immediately after the attack. Give the matter careful thought, and try to discover where you were weak and where you were fairly strong in fighting the attack. If you go into the matter

thoroughly you should be able to formulate rules for yourself to guide and help you should such an experience ever
come to you again.

SECTION FIFTY-THREE.

HOW TO CURE THE FEAR OF RIDICULE.

In considering the cure of ridicule it is necessary to
observe that there are three distinct mental attitudes
towards this fear. There is (1) that of the man who does
not care a rap about ridicule, (2) that of the man who
strives to avoid doing anything that will make him ridiculous, yet does not allow the thought of ridicule to worry
him, (3) that of the man who constantly fears doing anything, saying anything, or having attention drawn to himself, lest he appear ridiculous. Of these attitudes (1) and
(3) are wrong, and (2) is about right. (1) is wrong
because it is foolish to ignore ridicule: the man who ignores
ridicule is apt to do something ridiculous by his very attitude, and so to bring contempt upon himself. (3) is wrong
because it gives an undue prominence to ridicule: a man of
this type is taking the surest way to bring upon himself
that which he wishes to avoid.

Out of these three attitudes, there appears to spring this
general rule. Do nothing that will make you ridiculous,
but if through some error or oversight you should happen
to do something that will make you appear ridiculous, do
not let this worry you or overwhelm you. Make up your
mind that as far as possible you will not allow such a thing
to occur again; and next do all you can to minimize the
effects of the ridicule which you have brought upon yourself. Such a general rule will appeal to the common sense
of the ordinary man, but it will not do for the self-conscious
man. He requires leading up to the general rule by a

process of easy gradation, and therefore the following rules are for him, with that object in view.

RULE 1.—Get rid of the idea that whatever you do or say lays you open to ridicule from someone. Inhibit such thoughts the instant they enter your mind. Whatever you have to do concentrate upon doing it as well as possible; let this be your motto: "to do everything well," and it will keep your mind from foolish thoughts. Whatever you have to say, whether in conversation, or in business, or professional life, say it naturally without wondering whether it will make you ridiculous. Use prefunctioning or auto-suggestion if you fear any particular situation.

RULE 2.—Keep firmly in your mind the fact that ridicule always includes an element of criticism, and that the more ridiculous a person is the more he arouses our contempt for him. If you reflect upon this, you will gather that people are not anxious to see you making yourself ridiculous. They do not want you to be ridiculous—they want to see you at your best.

RULE 3.—To appear at your best before the world you must cultivate self-reliance, self-confidence, self-possession. You must be pleasant, mannerly, polite, courteous. You must always aim at doing things well and not keep wondering if people are criticizing your efforts. Adopt the view that your efforts will bear criticizing.

RULE 4.—If good-natured ridicule is directed against you, meet it by good nature. Remember that good-natured ridicule has no scorn or contempt behind it. It is not real ridicule; it may be prompted purely by fun or it may be intended to teach you important lessons which you will be wise to learn.

RULE 5.—If you have anything to do before the public, remember this—your audience has not come there with the idea of making you ridiculous; they want you to do well. They would rather that anything should happen than that you should do something that would make you ridiculous in their eyes.

RULE 6.—In doing anything in public, therefore, you will do well to put all thoughts of ridicule out of your mind. Be sure you CAN do what you have come to do, and you may be certain you will get your reward from the public, if you strive to do your best.

RULE 7.—Cultivate a sense of humor for it will help you in many an awkward situation and save you from ridicule, or at all events from the sting of ridicule.

SECTION FIFTY-FOUR.

HOW TO CURE THE FEAR OF THE LUDICROUS.

I feel sure that anyone who reads with care the analysis of this fear in *Section* 25 will require very little in the way of rules for its cure. It seems so clearly a matter for the exercise of common sense. The careful student of this book will see, however, that the self-conscious person is in a somewhat peculiar position. He is not devoid of common sense, but he is so much under the dominion of his emotions that they interfere with his reasoning powers.

The greatest failing of self-conscious people is their inability to grasp the essential difference between ridicule and the ludicrous. They are inclined to think of them as one and the same thing. If they will only try to remember that ridicule implies responsibility in the person exciting our ridicule, and that the ludicrous implies no responsibility, they will not need to worry over the fear of the ludicrous. Let me put this in another way. We speak of a person who excites our ridicule as a ridiculous person; we speak of a person who appears ludicrous as a ludicrous object. That is to say, his personality, his intelligence, character, etc., is never called in question; he is simply an object—a ludicrous object.   The following rules will, I trust, make this quite clear.

RULE 1.—Try to grasp that the fear of the ludicrous is a silly fear. YOU cannot make yourself ludicrous; it must be done by someone else, or something else, such as an accident over which you have no control.

RULE 2.—When you are so unfortunate as to be the principal character in a ludicrous situation, remember that no blame or responsibility attaches to you, therefore there is no need for you to worry. The spectators will not be slow; they will see the cause and will fix the blame on the right party, or right thing.

RULE 3.—The character in a ludicrous situation has always a feeling of embarrassment, quite apart from any sense of responsibility for the situation. Sometimes he suffers also from physical pain, but it is always the mental disturbance which causes him the greater pain. The attitude you must adopt in a situation like this is not that you have made a fool of yourself but simply that for the moment you are appearing in a wrong light, and that the matter will soon be righted. Try, therefore, to treat it lightly, good-humoredly, and you can rest assured you will have the sympathy and good feeling of the spectators. It is important that you should not give way to anger or vexation, for this will tend to make you ridiculous and thus alienate the sympathy and respect of those about you.

CHAPTER VIII.

THE NERVOUS TEMPERAMENT.

SECTION FIFTY-FIVE.

HOW TO CURE NERVOUSNESS.

In this section I have to consider four distinct types of nervousness, each of which will require separate treatment. These types are (1) People whose nervousness is due to fear traceable back to childhood, (2) people whose fear is due to a nervous temperament, (3) people whose nervousness is due to wrong living, (4) people who are suffering from neurasthenia.

I advise type (1) to study *Sections* 28, 29, 37, 46, 48, 49, 50, and put the rules in these sections into practice. Type (2) should read carefully my remarks relating to temperament in *Section* 26; and, as far as possible, try to moderate or subdue the prominent characteristics of the nervous temperament. Type (3) should study carefully the causes of non-temperamental nervousness, in *Section* 26; and those who are conscious that any of these causes applies to themselves should endeavor to remove them, and to order their lives afresh. Types (1), (2) and (3) should next carry out the advice, rules, and exercises which we give below. Type (4) should recognize that the wisest and safest plan is to put the case in the hands of a qualified nerve-specialist. There is no specific cure for neurasthenia, and no general rules can be given; each individual is a separate study to the nerve-specialist, and will require special treatment at his hands. Thus, he must endeavor to find to what faulty mental habits the symptoms of the case point; he has to combat the patient's morbid self-analysis and introspection; he has to consider what diet is most suitable, and what surroundings, and what form of rest are advisable. All this requires time and a great deal of painstaking work on the part of the nerve-specialist, and only he is qualified for such an undertaking.

(a) Don'ts For Nervous People.

1.—Don't pin your faith to quack remedies for nervousness, especially nerve-feeding foods; and foods to stimulate the brain. Your nerves and brain will get all the food they require from a good nourishing mixed diet. You cannot feed your nerves apart from your body; you can feed your nerves only by feeding your body as a whole. The same applies to the brain. If you feel you MUST have something other than your ordinary food buy some sweets or chocolates and eat them after your meals.

2.—Don't touch alcoholic drinks or narcotics; if you must have a stimulant take a cup of tea, which should be of good quality and not infused longer than two or three minutes. As regards the use of tobacco, there is no general agreement on the subject. If you can do without it, do so; if you cannot, use it in strict moderation.

3.—Don't think that faith-healing, hypnotism, or any other form of suggestion ALONE will cure you. They are excellent in their place but you must remember that nervousness always implies impaired nutrition. To cure it, therefore, you must first build up your body, and then mental methods of healing will have a proper chance to do their work.

4.—Don't go in for exercise of a tiring or exciting character. Consult your doctor before you engage in games like cricket or football, and recreation such as golf and motoring. Walking is the best exercise, but unless you can take an interest in your walks they will not do you much good. Practice breathing exercises when out in the street so as to get the full value from your walk.

5.—Don't try to keep too many irons in the fire—it leads to excitement and worry.

6.—Don't do your work by fits and starts, and in work I include your hobbies and studies. Be regular: irregularity in work or study is harmful to the nerves.

7.—Don't think that hard work will kill you. A man can work for a very long time if he steers clear of worry and excitement. If you can see your work progressing and yourself making steady advancement you will stimulate your nerves and enjoy life.

8.—Don't dwell on thoughts that annoy you or cause you trouble, for this leads to worry. Wait until your mind is quieter and then think things out calmly and quietly. Be methodical in dealing with difficulties; go from point to point quietly and steadily until you can see light ahead.

9.—Don't talk loudly or quickly either at home or abroad. Cultivate an even, quiet, steady tone of voice and you will help your nerves greatly.

10.—Don't rush along the streets as if you were always hurrying to catch a train, and don't rush through your work at a feverish pace. Conserve your energy and you will strengthen your nerves.

11.—Don't swallow your meals at a gulp. Eat leisurely and masticate your food thoroughly and in this way you WILL feed your nerves.

12.—Don't talk to other people about your nervousness—its symptoms, its effects upon your health, its worries, or the remedies you have tried or are trying. To talk to other people about your trouble will only intensify it, and make it harder to bear and harder to cure.

(b) Rules For Nervous People.

RULE 1.—Study carefully *Section* 26 and see if you can discover the cause of your nervousness. As soon as you find the cause, resolve that you will do all in your power to remove it. The instruction given in this section will help you.

RULE 2.—Practice the ideas given in *Sections* 30 to 35, but do everything very gradually and very gently. There must be absolutely no sense of strain.

RULE 3.—Live by rule. Map out your day and stick to your time-table, as far as possible. Regularity of life is of the utmost importance to you. Go to bed at a fixed hour each day, and rise at a set time. Never indulge in extra naps in the morning; they are very bad for nervous people. If you possibly can, get to bed by ten or eleven o'clock at the latest each night, and get up when you waken. Nature will soon regulate matters if you are punctual in going to bed at a fixed time each night.

RULE 4.—Get away from everything and everybody for an hour each day. After lunch is the best time, but unfortunately this is not always possible for the majority of people. Lie down and rest (do not confound this with exercise 1 below). If you drop off to sleep, so much the better; if you cannot manage this, read a light book, one that is not overstimulating nor too dry.

(c) EXERCISES FOR NERVOUS PEOPLE.

Exercise 1.—Lie down on a bed, or a couch, with your head and feet at the same level (*i.e.*, use no pillows or cushions for the head). Close your eyes and stretch out your legs to their full extent. After a few seconds raise each leg separately, and let it fall. Do not attempt to move it after it falls; let it lie exactly where it falls. Do the same with each arm separately—stretch it by the side to its full extent, next raise it about two feet in the air, and then let it fall, to rest where it falls. Next raise the head a few inches and then let it fall back to rest where it falls. Try now to feel that all the muscles in your body are relaxed and that there is not the slightest feeling of strain. Rest in this way for five minutes. Practice this exercise morning and evening each day, and also when you feel tired and worn out.

Exercise 2.—After practicing the above exercise for a few times try to combine with it the following exercise. While you are lying resting, perfectly relaxed, try to relax your mind. Stop thinking of business, or your profession, or any of your daily activities. Stop thinking of your hobbies, studies, amusements, news of the day, or any thoughts of a worrying nature. Simply feel that you are resting mind and body. Try for the time being to feel that you are resting, resting, and that nothing else matters for the moment.

Exercise 3.—If you are in business, or in a profession, try the following relaxation exercise. It is one I can thoroughly recommend, for I have practiced it myself for many years and have learned to estimate its value. As soon as you leave your shop or office, at the hour of lunch or at the close of the day's work, relax your mind by encouraging the feeling that you are free, free, free; free from the strain of your work. Try to feel that you have nothing to do now. You are having a holiday and are going to enjoy yourself. Inhibit thoughts of your work, and think nothing but thoughts of freedom, joy, and pleasure. Put this feeling into your steps as you walk along the street. Look at passers-by pleasantly, and continue to feel that you are free, free from all strain and anxiety. I can assure you that even a few minutes spent in this way works wonders as a mental tonic. If you put this exercise into practice, you will go back to your work a new man, and much fitter to grapple with difficulties, or petty annoyances and worries.

SECTION FIFTY-SIX.

HOW TO CURE FEARS PERTAINING TO ADOLESCENCE.

It will be understood from what I have said in *Section* 27 that the fears pertaining to adolescence all center round the functional changes which take place at that period, viz., from the age of twelve years in the case of girls, and from the ages of fourteen and fifteen years in the case of boys. Of these changes the pubertal change (*i.e.*, as marking the development of the generative powers) is responsible for most of the adolescent fears, and the mental distress or disturbance. The years of greatest stress are naturally the early years of the period. In school life, the stress at once affects the mental activities of the pupils; some pupils become brilliant, and others grow dull. In social life both sexes tend to become timid, shy, or bashful; in some cases the tendency is slight, and only shows itself on special occasions; in other cases the tendency is pronounced, until it becomes apparent at all times. In the religious life the stress is marked by doubt, perplexity, and the heightening of the imagination, hence it is not astonishing, as Prof. Starbuck points out in his "PSYCHOLOGY OF RELIGION," that "conversion belongs almost exclusively to the years between ten and twenty-five."

The early years of the adolescent period are the most important in relation to self-consciousness. Boys and girls are apt to dwell upon the disturbing elements that have come into their life until their constantly repeated thoughts become obsessions and permanently affect their lives. I must, therefore, in laying down rules, divide the adolescent period into two parts—the early years of adolescence and the later years of adolescence—and give separate rules for each.

I cannot enter here into the vexed question of sexual instruction to boys and girls. My rules are given on the assumption that at least some knowledge of this has been acquired, either from teachers or parents, or from reading, especially as regards the pubertal change.

(*a*) RULES FOR THE EARLY YEARS OF ADOLESCENCE.

RULE 1.—When you begin to realize that your voice is changing, do not worry if you are chaffed about it. Try to grasp that this change of voice is natural and merely a transition stage in your life, and that the difference in tone which you and your friends notice is purely a temporary matter and will soon cease to attract notice. Do not keep thinking of it; inhibit such tendency AT ONCE. Realize that there is nothing mysterious about the vocal change; it comes to everyone—all your adult friends have been affected by it without anything dreadful happening.

RULE 2.—When you begin to feel you are "all legs and arms," that is to say, when you begin to be conscious that your movements are awkward, dismiss such thoughts at once. Do not dwell on them or allow them to worry you; nature will soon put you all right. If anyone speaks to you chaffingly about the matter, laugh it off; recognize that it is not worth troubling about.

RULE 3.—When you feel a tendency to shrink from meeting people or a tendency to avoid people, fight the feeling at once. It all springs from thinking of yourself, and is common with young people at your age, and if you give way to the feeling it will work havoc in your life. Go forward; meet people pleasantly and never mind a little chaff if it is given; be genial and good mannered and you will soon feel at your ease. Never mind an occasional failure—fight the tendency to avoid people and you will speedily overcome it. Make the fight NOW, and you will save yourself a great deal of annoyance in after life.

RULE 4.—Fight the tendency to be shy, timid, or bashful when in the presence of young people of opposite sex. It is a common tendency at your age and a resolute attempt must be made to overcome it. Go into such company fearlessly and boldly, taking care to observe all the essentials of good breeding. Be courteous, polite, frank and agreeable, and conform to all the requirements of good taste and propriety.

RULE 5.—Resist any tendency to depression and lowness of spirits. Such feelings are very common in the early years of adolescence. You get thinking of your body, you imagine you are in the grip of serious complaints, you have horrible dreams and feel sure you will not live long. Inhibit such thoughts at once, otherwise they will develop into numerous fears. Any doctor will tell you that such thoughts are simply nonsense, therefore, do not dwell on them for a single moment. Get out in the open air, take plenty of exercise, go into cheerful company, and try to forget you have such a thing as a body. Simulate joy and happiness until you begin to feel their tonic effects. Keep the mind busy with bright, cheery, merry thoughts, and laughter, and your fits of depression will soon take flight.

RULE 6.—Hold fast to the faith and belief which you think is best suited for the furthering of your mental and physical well being. Let faith in Self be a guiding principle in your life. Recognize that faith in Self develops Self, and that Self development without absolute faith and belief in Self is impossible. Faith in Self for health begets health, and health, without belief and faith in health, is unobtainable. What you believe, and what you found your faith upon is manifested in you mentally and physically. It is an immutable law, of Nature, that what you believe in shall be manifested in your life. Believe in things desirable and your life will express them. Make yourself positive against the undesirable things of life, and this mental attitude will exclude them from your existence; and you will thereby become immune to those things which wreck and ruin man's physical existence.

(b) RULES FOR THE LATER YEARS OF ADOLESCENCE.

RULE 1.—If you are conscious that by allowing your mind to dwell too much upon thoughts of self, incidental to the changes that came into your life in the earlier years of adolescence, you have become shy, timid, or bashful, you must practice diligently the rules contained in *Sections* 48 to 50.

RULE 2.—If you are troubled with blushing, try to grasp that it is very common to your period of life and can be overcome if you will set yourself seriously to grapple with it. Practice the rules given in *Section* 52 and try to add to these rules yourself so as to meet special situations or occasions in your life. The guiding principle of each rule must be the getting your mind away from thoughts of self. In talking to anyone you must never think of yourself nor of what others may be thinking of you. Center all your thoughts on the person to whom you are talking, and you will find that you will not be so liable to blush.

RULE 3.—Recognize that at your time of life the fear of ridicule and the fear of the ludicrous are specially liable to attack you. Adults know this, and some of your companions are sure to know it, and will be inclined to use this knowledge against you. Do all you can to fight such fears. Practice the rules given in *Section* 53 and *Section* 54, and you will have little to fear from such attacks.

RULE 4.—It is of the greatest importance that you should begin now to cultivate a strong belief in yourself. Some young people at your age have an erroneous idea of what this means. They think that belief in self means the belief that one can do anything he tries to do. Guard against this. Recognize your limitations, but wherever it is possible, try to remove them. Be a severe critic of yourself, and then what you really think you CAN do, do it with all your might. Practice the rules given in *Section* 37.

RULE 5.—A common feeling at your age is the fear of entering on a new stage of life. This is specially prominent when you enter business life. Read carefully my remarks in *Section* 45, and practice the rules where they apply to you. From the beginning of your business career, make it your constant effort to fight the particular fears that beset you. Cultivate a strong belief in your power to overcome every obstacle, and make and use affirmations to this end. Do not let anything daunt you; where you lack knowledge do all you can to gain it; you will find the way to do it if you are in earnest, and you must be in earnest in the business world of to-day.

RULE 6.—If you are conscious that you are of a nervous temperament you must do all you can to fight against its excesses and extravagances. Make your temperament work FOR you instead of against you. The rules and hints given in *Section* 55 will help you.

NOTE.—I strongly advise young men and young women to get a good grip of the following sections in this book; they are of the greatest importance to them if they are to do themselves justice in the battle of life. *Sections* 8, 14, 15, **16**, *Sections* 18 to 37, *Sections* 43 to 45, *Sections* 48 to 55.

Printed in the United States
64607LVS00005B/41